Meditations

Selections from Bahá'í Scripture

Bahá'í
PUBLISHING
Wilmette, Illinois

Bahá'í Publishing, 401 Greenleaf Avenue,
Wilmette IL 60091-2844
 Published 2008
Printed in the United States of America on acid-free paper ∞

16 15 14 13 4 3 2

Library of Congress Cataloging-in-Publication Data
Meditations : selections from Bahá'í Scripture.
p. cm.
Includes bibliographical references and index.
ISBN-13: 978-1-931847-56-8
ISBN-10: 1-931847-56-8
1. Bahai Faith—Prayers and devotions. I. Bahá'í Publishing
Trust.

BP380.B35 2008
297.9'3432—dc22

2007049285

Cover and book design by Suni D. Hannan

Meditations

Blessed are they that
remember the one true God,
that magnify His Name,
and seek diligently to serve His Cause.
—BAHÁ'U'LLÁH

Contents

Preface *ix*

Passages for Meditation *1*

List of Abbreviations *149*

References *151*

Bibliography *159*

Preface

Among the teachings of Bahá'u'lláh, Whom millions of people around the world believe to be the Messenger of God for today, is that our primary purpose in life is to know and to love God. In the Bahá'í Faith, as in every religion, prayer and meditation are fundamental tools for spiritual development. Through the daily practice of prayer, we commune with God and sustain and strengthen our souls. Through daily meditation, Bahá'u'lláh writes, "the secret of things unseen" is revealed and "the sweetness of a spiritual and imperishable fragrance" is inhaled.

The Bahá'í scriptures are a source of light and inspiration for the soul. They are like an endless ocean whose depths we cannot fathom but into whose mysteries we can dive again and again to discover new pearls of wisdom and understanding. This collection of meditative passages is compiled from the writings of Bahá'u'lláh, as well as from those of His forerunner, the Báb, and those of His son and appointed successor, 'Abdu'l-Bahá. The readings assembled here provide only a small sampling of the vast body of Bahá'í writings available in English. It is hoped that these passages will inspire the reader to delve more deeply into the works from which they were selected.

1

The appearances of the Manifestations of God are the divine springtime. When Christ appeared in this world, it was like the vernal bounty; the outpouring descended; the effulgences of the Merciful encircled all things; the human world found new life. Even the physical world partook of it. The divine perfections were upraised; souls were trained in the school of heaven so that all grades of human existence received life and light. Then by degrees these fragrances of heaven were discontinued; the season of winter came upon the world; the beauties of spring vanished; the excellences and perfections passed away; the lights and quickening were no longer evident; the phenomenal world and its materialities conquered everything; the spiritualities of life were lost; the world of existence became life unto a lifeless body; there was no trace of the spring left.

Bahá'u'lláh has come into this world. He has renewed that springtime. The same fragrances are wafting; the same heat of the Sun is giving life; the same cloud is pouring its rain, and with our own eyes we see that the world of existence is advancing and progressing. The human world has found new life.

—*'Abdu'l-Bahá*

2

At the time of the vernal equinox in the material world a wonderful vibrant energy and new life-quickening is observed everywhere in the vegetable kingdom; the animal and human kingdoms are resuscitated and move forward with a new impulse. The whole world is born anew, resurrected. Gentle zephyrs are set in motion, wafting and fragrant; flowers bloom; the trees are in blossom, the air temperate and delightful; how pleasant and beautiful become the mountains, fields and meadows. Likewise, the spiritual bounty and springtime of God quicken the world of humanity with a new animus and vivification. All the virtues which have been deposited and potential in human hearts are being revealed from that Reality as flowers and blossoms from divine gardens. It is a day of joy, a time of happiness, a period of spiritual growth.

—*'Abdu'l-Bahá*

3

O friends! It behooveth you to refresh and revive your souls through the gracious favors which in this Divine, this soul-stirring Springtime are being showered upon you. The Daystar of His great glory hath shed its radiance upon you, and the clouds of His limitless grace have overshadowed you. How high the reward of him who hath not deprived himself of so great a bounty, nor failed to recognize the beauty of his Best-Beloved in this, His new attire.

—*Bahá'u'lláh*

4

How numerous are those peoples of divers beliefs, of conflicting creeds, and opposing temperaments, who, through the reviving fragrance of the Divine springtime . . . have been arrayed with the new robe of divine Unity, and have drunk from the cup of His singleness!

This is the significance of the well-known words: "The wolf and the lamb shall feed together."

—*Bahá'u'lláh*

5

Consort with the followers of all religions in a spirit of friendliness and fellowship. . . .

They that are endued with sincerity and faithfulness should associate with all the peoples and kindreds of the earth with joy and radiance, inasmuch as consorting with people hath promoted and will continue to promote unity and concord, which in turn are conducive to the maintenance of order in the world and to the regeneration of nations.

—*Bahá'u'lláh*

6

There can be no doubt whatever that the peoples of the world, of whatever race or religion, derive their inspiration from one heavenly Source, and are the subjects of one God.

—*Bahá'u'lláh*

7

What profit is there in agreeing that universal friendship is good, and talking of the solidarity of the human race as a grand ideal? Unless these thoughts are translated into the world of action, they are useless.

—*'Abdu'l-Bahá*

8

Put into practice the Teaching of Bahá'u'lláh, that of kindness to all nations. Do not be content with showing friendship in words alone, let your heart burn with loving kindness for all who may cross your path.

—*'Abdu'l-Bahá*

9

The wrong in the world continues to exist just because people talk only of their ideals, and do not strive to put them into practice. If actions took the place of words, the world's misery would very soon be changed into comfort.

—*'Abdu'l-Bahá*

10

O ye beloved of the Lord! Commit not that which defileth the limpid stream of love or destroyeth the sweet fragrance of friendship. By the righteousness of the Lord! Ye were created to show love one to another and not perversity and rancor. Take pride not in love for yourselves but in love for your fellow-creatures. Glory not in love for your country, but in love for all mankind. Let your eye be chaste, your hand faithful, your tongue truthful and your heart enlightened.

—*Bahá'u'lláh*

11

The Prophets and Chosen Ones have all been commissioned by the One True God, magnified be His glory, to nurture the trees of human existence with the living waters of uprightness and understanding, that there may appear from them that which God hath deposited within their inmost selves. As may be readily observed, each tree yieldeth a certain fruit, and a barren tree is but fit for fire. The purpose of these Educators, in all they said and taught, was to preserve man's exalted station.

—*Bahá'u'lláh*

12

Say: O children of dust! He Who is the Spirit of Purity saith: In this glorious Day whatsoever can purge you from defilement and ensure your peace and tranquillity, that indeed is the straight Path, the Path that leadeth unto Me. To be purged from defilement is to be cleansed of that which is injurious to man and detracteth from his high station—among which is to take undue pleasure in one's own words and deeds, notwithstanding their unworthiness. True peace and tranquillity will only be realized when every soul will have become the well-wisher of all mankind.

—*Bahá'u'lláh*

13

Do not complain of others. Refrain from reprimanding them, and if you wish to give admonition or advice, let it be offered in such a way that it will not burden the bearer.

—*'Abdu'l-Bahá*

14

Pray thou that the ill-natured become good-natured and the weak become strong.

—'Abdu'l-Bahá

15

Beautify your tongues, O people, with truthfulness, and adorn your souls with the ornament of honesty. Beware, O people, that ye deal not treacherously with anyone. Be ye the trustees of God amongst His creatures, and the emblems of His generosity amidst His people. They that follow their lusts and corrupt inclinations, have erred and dissipated their efforts. They, indeed, are of the lost. Strive, O people, that your eyes may be directed towards the mercy of God, that your hearts may be attuned to His wondrous remembrance, that your souls may rest confidently upon His grace and bounty, that your feet may tread the path of His good-pleasure.

—Bahá'u'lláh

16

Beware lest the desires of the flesh and of a corrupt inclination provoke divisions among you. Be ye as the fingers of one hand, the members of one body.

—Bahá'u'lláh

17

The utterance of God is a lamp, whose light is these words: Ye are the fruits of one tree, and the leaves of one branch. Deal ye one with another with the utmost love and harmony, with friendliness and fellowship. He Who is the Daystar of Truth beareth Me witness! So powerful is the light of unity that it can illuminate the whole earth. The One true God, He Who knoweth all things, Himself testifieth to the truth of these words.

—*Baha'u'llah*

18

This is the Day in which God's most excellent favors have been poured out upon men, the Day in which His most mighty grace hath been infused into all created things. It is incumbent upon all the peoples of the world to reconcile their differences, and, with perfect unity and peace, abide beneath the shadow of the Tree of His care and loving-kindness. It behooveth them to cleave to whatsoever will, in this Day, be conducive to the exaltation of their stations, and to the promotion of their best interests. Happy are those whom the all-glorious Pen was moved to remember, and blessed are those men whose names, by virtue of Our inscrutable decree, We have preferred to conceal.

Beseech ye the one true God to grant that all men may be graciously assisted to fulfill that which is acceptable in Our sight. Soon will the present-day order be rolled up, and a new one spread out in its stead. Verily, thy Lord speaketh the truth, and is the Knower of things unseen.

—*Bahá'u'lláh*

19

It is Our wish and desire that every one of you may become a source of all goodness unto men, and an example of uprightness to mankind. Beware lest ye prefer yourselves above your neighbors.

—*Bahá'u'lláh*

20

O ye loved ones of the Lord! This is the hour when ye must associate with all the earth's peoples in extreme kindliness and love, and be to them the signs and tokens of God's great mercy.

—*'Abdu'l-Bahá*

21

The sword of a virtuous character and upright conduct is sharper than blades of steel.

—*Bahá'u'lláh*

22

O people of God! Do not busy yourselves in your own concerns; let your thoughts be fixed upon that which will rehabilitate the fortunes of mankind and sanctify the hearts and souls of men. This can best be achieved through pure and holy deeds, through a virtuous life and a goodly behavior.

—Bahá'u'lláh

23

Religion concerns matters of the heart, of the spirit, and of morals.

Politics are occupied with the material things of life. Religious teachers should not invade the realm of politics; they should concern themselves with the spiritual education of the people; they should ever give good counsel to men, trying to serve God and humankind; they should endeavor to awaken spiritual aspiration, and strive to enlarge the understanding and knowledge of humanity, to improve morals, and to increase the love for justice.

This is in accordance with the Teaching of Bahá'u'lláh.

—'Abdu'l-Bahá

24

Human happiness is founded upon spiritual behavior.

—*'Abdu'l-Bahá*

25

The Great Being saith: O ye children of men! The fundamental purpose animating the Faith of God and His Religion is to safeguard the interests and promote the unity of the human race, and to foster the spirit of love and fellowship amongst men. Suffer it not to become a source of dissension and discord, of hate and enmity. This is the straight Path, the fixed and immovable foundation. Whatsoever is raised on this foundation, the changes and chances of the world can never impair its strength, nor will the revolution of countless centuries undermine its structure.

—*Bahá'u'lláh*

26

Every human creature is the servant of God. All have been created and reared by the power and favor of God; all have been blessed with the bounties of the same Sun of divine truth; all have quaffed from the fountain of the infinite mercy of God; and all in His estimation and love are equal as servants. He is beneficent and kind to all.

—'Abdu'l-Bahá

27

O Son of Being!

Bring thyself to account each day ere thou art summoned to a reckoning; for death, unheralded, shall come upon thee and thou shalt be called to give account for thy deeds.

—Bahá'u'lláh

28

O Thou Whose nearness is my wish, Whose presence is my hope, Whose remembrance is my desire, Whose court of glory is my goal, Whose abode is my aim, Whose name is my healing, Whose love is the radiance of my heart, Whose service is my highest aspiration! I beseech Thee by Thy Name, through which Thou hast enabled them that have recognized Thee to soar to the sublimest heights of the knowledge of Thee and empowered such as devoutly worship Thee to ascend into the precincts of the court of Thy holy favors, to aid me to turn my face towards Thy face, to fix mine eyes upon Thee, and to speak of Thy glory.

—Bahá'u'lláh

29

O Son of Spirit!
There is no peace for thee save by renouncing thyself and turning unto Me; for it behooveth thee to glory in My name, not in thine own; to put thy trust in Me and not in thyself, since I desire to be loved alone and above all that is.

—*Bahá'u'lláh*

30

Never lose thy trust in God. Be thou ever hopeful, for the bounties of God never cease to flow upon man. If viewed from one perspective they seem to decrease, but from another they are full and complete. Man is under all conditions immersed in a sea of God's blessings. Therefore, be thou not hopeless under any circumstances, but rather be firm in thy hope.

—*'Abdu'l-Bahá*

31

Grief and sorrow do not come to us by chance, they are sent to us by the Divine Mercy for our own perfecting.

While a man is happy he may forget his God; but when grief comes and sorrows overwhelm him, then will he remember his Father who is in Heaven, and who is able to deliver him from his humiliations.

—*'Abdu'l-Bahá*

32

God is merciful. In His mercy He answers the prayers of all His servants when according to His supreme wisdom it is necessary.

—*'Abdu'l-Bahá*

33

Having created the world and all that liveth and moveth therein, He, through the direct operation of His unconstrained and sovereign Will, chose to confer upon man the unique distinction and capacity to know Him and to love Him—a capacity that must needs be regarded as the generating impulse and the primary purpose underlying the whole of creation.

—*Bahá'u'lláh*

34

Humility exalteth man to the heaven of glory and power, whilst pride abaseth him to the depths of wretchedness and degradation.

—*Bahá'u'lláh*

35

O Oppressors on Earth!
Withdraw your hands from tyranny, for I have pledged Myself not to forgive any man's injustice.

This is My covenant which I have irrevocably decreed in the preserved tablet and sealed with My seal of glory.

—*Bahá'u'lláh*

36

Delight not yourselves in the things of the world and its vain ornaments, neither set your hopes on them. Let your reliance be on the remembrance of God, the Most Exalted, the Most Great.

—*Bahá'u'lláh*

37

Attract the hearts of men, through the call of Him, the one alone Beloved. Say: This is the Voice of God, if ye do but hearken. This is the Dayspring of the Revelation of God, did ye but know it. This is the Dawning-Place of the Cause of God, were ye to recognize it. This is the Source of the commandment of God, did ye but judge it fairly.

—*Bahá'u'lláh*

38

Be fair to yourselves and to others, that the evidences of justice may be revealed, through your deeds, among Our faithful servants. Beware lest ye encroach upon the substance of your neighbor. Prove yourselves worthy of his trust and confidence in you, and withhold not from the poor the gifts which the grace of God hath bestowed upon you. He, verily, shall recompense the charitable, and doubly repay them for what they have bestowed.

—*Bahá'u'lláh*

39

Consider the influence of the sun upon the earthly beings, what signs and results become evident and clear from its nearness and remoteness, from its rising or its setting. At one time it is autumn, at another time spring; or again it is summer or winter. When the sun passes the line of the equator, the life-giving spring will become manifest in splendor, and when it is in the summer solstice, the fruits will attain to the acme of perfection, grains and plants will yield their produce, and earthly beings will attain their most complete development and growth.

In like manner, when the Holy Manifestation of God, Who is the sun of the world of His creation, shines upon the worlds of spirits, of thoughts and of hearts, then the spiritual spring and new life appear, the power of the wonderful springtime becomes visible, and marvelous benefits are apparent. As you have observed, at the time of the appearance of each Manifestation of God extraordinary progress has occurred in the world of minds, thoughts and spirits.

—*'Abdu'l-Bahá*

40

Verily, He Who is the Spirit of Truth is come to guide you unto all truth. He speaketh not as prompted by His own self, but as bidden by Him Who is the All-Knowing, the All-Wise.

Say, this is the One Who hath glorified the Son and hath exalted His Cause. Cast away, O peoples of the earth, that which ye have and take fast hold of that which ye are bidden by the All-Powerful, He Who is the Bearer of the Trust of God. Purge ye your ears and set your hearts towards Him that ye may hearken to the most wondrous Call which hath been raised from Sinai, the habitation of your Lord, the Most Glorious. It will, in truth, draw you nigh unto the Spot wherein ye will perceive the splendor of the light of His countenance which shineth above this luminous Horizon.

—*Bahá'u'lláh*

41

Suffer me not, O my Lord, to be deprived of the knowledge of Thee in Thy days, and divest me not of the robe of Thy guidance. Give me to drink of the river that is life indeed, whose waters have streamed forth from the Paradise (Riḍvan) in which the throne of Thy Name, the All-Merciful, was established, that mine eyes may be opened, and my face be illumined, and my heart be assured, and my soul be enlightened, and my steps be made firm.

—*Bahá'u'lláh*

42

Consort with all men, O people of Bahá,* in a spirit of friendliness and fellowship. If ye be aware of a certain truth, if ye possess a jewel, of which others are deprived, share it with them in a language of utmost kindliness and goodwill. If it be accepted, if it fulfill its purpose, your object is attained. If anyone should refuse it, leave him unto himself, and beseech God to guide him. Beware lest ye deal unkindly with him. A kindly tongue is the lodestone of the hearts of men. It is the bread of the spirit, it clotheth the words with meaning, it is the fountain of the light of wisdom and understanding. . . .

—*Bahá'u'lláh*

* The term "people of Bahá" refers to the followers of Bahá'u'lláh.

43

Become as true brethren in the one and indivisible religion of God, free from distinction, for verily God desireth that your hearts should become mirrors unto your brethren in the Faith, so that ye find yourselves reflected in them, and they in you. This is the true Path of God, the Almighty, and He is indeed watchful over your actions.

—*The Báb*

44

The fact that we imagine ourselves to be right and everybody else wrong is the greatest of all obstacles in the path towards unity, and unity is necessary if we would reach truth, for truth is *one.*

—*'Abdu'l-Bahá*

45

God sent His Prophets into the world to teach and enlighten man, to explain to him the mystery of the Power of the Holy Spirit, to enable him to reflect the light, and so in his turn, to be the source of guidance to others.

—*'Abdu'l-Bahá*

46

O God! Sanctify me from all else save Thee, purge me from the dross of sins and transgressions, and cause me to possess a spiritual heart and conscience.

Verily, Thou art merciful and, verily, Thou art the Most Generous, Whose help is sought by all men.

—*'Abdu'l-Bahá*

47

This is the Day whereon the Ocean of God's mercy hath been manifested unto men, the Day in which the Daystar of His loving-kindness hath shed its radiance upon them, the Day in which the clouds of His bountiful favor have overshadowed the whole of mankind. Now is the time to cheer and refresh the down-cast through the invigorating breeze of love and fellowship, and the living waters of friendliness and charity.

—*Bahá'u'lláh*

48

Verily I say, this is the Day in which mankind can behold the Face, and hear the Voice, of the Promised One. The Call of God hath been raised, and the light of His countenance hath been lifted up upon men. It behooveth every man to blot out the trace of every idle word from the tablet of his heart, and to gaze, with an open and unbiased mind, on the signs of His Revelation, the proofs of His Mission, and the tokens of His glory.

—*Bahá'u'lláh*

49

My God, my Adored One, my King, my Desire! What tongue can voice my thanks to Thee? I was heedless, Thou didst awaken me. I had turned back from Thee, Thou didst graciously aid me to turn towards Thee. I was as one dead, Thou didst quicken me with the water of life. I was withered, Thou didst revive me with the heavenly stream of Thine utterance which hath flowed forth from the Pen of the All-Merciful.

—*Bahá'u'lláh*

50

O peoples of the world! Cast away, in My name that transcendeth all other names, the things ye possess, and immerse yourselves in this Ocean in whose depths lay hidden the pearls of wisdom and of utterance, an ocean that surgeth in My name, the All-Merciful.

—*Bahá'u'lláh*

51

I was but a man like others, asleep upon My couch, when lo, the breezes of the All-Glorious were wafted over Me, and taught Me the knowledge of all that hath been. This thing is not from Me, but from One Who is Almighty and All-Knowing. . . . His all-compelling summons hath reached Me, and caused Me to speak His praise amidst all people. I was indeed as one dead when His behest was uttered. The hand of the will of thy Lord, the Compassionate, the Merciful, transformed Me.

—*Bahá'u'lláh*

52

The first bestowal of God is the Word, and its discoverer and recipient is the power of understanding. This Word is the foremost instructor in the school of existence and the revealer of Him Who is the Almighty. All that is seen is visible only through the light of its wisdom. All that is manifest is but a token of its knowledge. All names are but its name, and the beginning and end of all matters must needs depend upon it.

—*Bahá'u'lláh*

53

O Son of the Throne!
Thy hearing is My hearing, hear thou therewith. Thy sight is My sight, do thou see therewith, that in thine inmost soul thou mayest testify unto My

exalted sanctity, and I within Myself may bear witness unto an exalted station for thee.

—*Bahá'u'lláh*

54

The source of all learning is the knowledge of God, exalted be His Glory, and this cannot be attained save through the knowledge of His Divine Manifestation.

—*Bahá'u'lláh*

55

We, verily, have not fallen short of Our duty to exhort men, and to deliver that whereunto I was bidden by God, the Almighty, the All-Praised.

—*Bahá'u'lláh*

56

Is there any excuse left for any one in this Revelation? No, by God, the Lord of the Mighty Throne! My signs have encompassed the earth, and my power enveloped all mankind.

—*Bahá'u'lláh*

57

It is clear and evident that whenever the Manifestations of Holiness were revealed, the divines of their day have hindered the people from attaining unto the way of truth. To this testify the records of all the scriptures and heavenly books. Not one Prophet of God was made manifest Who did not fall a victim to the relentless hate, to the denunciation, denial, and execration of the clerics of His day!

—Bahá'u'lláh

58

One night, in a dream, these exalted words were heard on every side: "Verily, We shall render Thee victorious by Thyself and by Thy Pen. Grieve Thou not for that which hath befallen Thee, neither be Thou afraid, for Thou art in safety. Erelong will God raise up the treasures of the earth—men who will aid Thee through Thyself and through Thy Name, wherewith God hath revived the hearts of such as have recognized Him."

—Bahá'u'lláh

59

Let deeds, not words, be your adorning.

—Bahá'u'lláh

60

God, who sees all hearts, knows how far our lives are the fulfillment of our words.

—'Abdu'l-Bahá

61

No man shall attain the shores of the ocean of true understanding except he be detached from all that is in heaven and on earth. Sanctify your souls, O ye peoples of the world, that haply ye may attain that station which God hath destined for you. . . .

—*Bahá'u'lláh*

62

They that tread the path of faith, they that thirst for the wine of certitude, must cleanse themselves of all that is earthly—their ears from idle talk, their minds from vain imaginings, their hearts from worldly affections, their eyes from that which perisheth. They should put their trust in God, and, holding fast unto Him, follow in His way. Then will they be made worthy of the effulgent glories of the sun of divine knowledge and understanding, and become the recipients of a grace that is infinite and unseen, inasmuch as man can never hope to attain unto the knowledge of the All-Glorious, can never quaff from the stream of divine knowledge and wisdom, can never enter the abode of immortality, nor partake of the cup of divine nearness and favor, unless and until he ceases to regard the words and deeds of mortal men as a standard for the true understanding and recognition of God and His Prophets.

—*Bahá'u'lláh*

63

He Who is the sovereign Lord of all is come. The Kingdom is God's, the omnipotent Protector, the Self-Subsisting. Worship none but God, and, with radiant hearts, lift up your faces unto your Lord, the Lord of all names. This is a Revelation to which whatever ye possess can never be compared, could ye but know it.

—*Bahá'u'lláh*

64

O Pope! Rend the veils asunder. He Who is the Lord of Lords is come overshadowed with clouds, and the decree hath been fulfilled by God, the Almighty, the Unrestrained. . . . He, verily, hath again come down from Heaven even as He came down from it the first time.

—*Bahá'u'lláh*

65

O concourse of monks! Seclude not yourselves in your churches and cloisters. Come ye out of them by My leave, and busy, then, yourselves with what will profit you and others. Thus commandeth you He Who is the Lord of the Day of Reckoning. Seclude yourselves in the stronghold of My love. This, truly, is the seclusion that befitteth you, could ye but know it.

—*Bahá'u'lláh*

66

O Son of Man!
Veiled in My immemorial being and in the ancient eternity of My essence, I knew My love for thee; therefore I created thee, have engraved on thee Mine image and revealed to thee My beauty.

—*Bahá'u'lláh*

67

They who are possessed of riches . . . must have the utmost regard for the poor, for great is the honor destined by God for those poor who are steadfast in patience. By My life! There is no honor, except what God may please to bestow, that can compare to this honor. Great is the blessedness awaiting the poor that endure patiently and conceal their sufferings, and well is it with the rich who bestow their riches on the needy and prefer them before themselves.

—Bahá'u'lláh

68

Blessed is he who preferreth his brother before himself.

—*Bahá'u'lláh*

69

O friends! Be not careless of the virtues with which ye have been endowed, neither be neglectful of your high destiny. Suffer not your labors to be wasted through the vain imaginations which certain hearts have devised. Ye are the stars of the heaven of understanding, the breeze that stirreth at the break of day, the soft-flowing waters upon which must depend the very life of all men, the letters inscribed upon His sacred scroll.

—*Bahá'u'lláh*

70

The essence of charity is for the servant to recount the blessings of his Lord, and to render thanks unto Him at all times and under all conditions.

—*Bahá'u'lláh*

71

Pray to God that thou mayest become . . . a lover of men and a well-wisher of humankind.

—*'Abdu'l-Bahá*

72

Arise O people, and, by the power of God's might, resolve to gain the victory over your own selves, that haply the whole earth may be freed and sanctified from its servitude to the gods of its idle fancies—gods that have inflicted such loss upon, and are responsible for the misery of, their wretched worshippers.

—*Bahá'u'lláh*

73

Consider the former generations. Witness how every time the Daystar of Divine bounty hath shed the light of His Revelation upon the world, the people of His Day have arisen against Him, and repudiated His truth. They who were regarded as the leaders of men have invariably striven to hinder their followers from turning unto Him Who is the Ocean of God's limitless bounty.

—*Bahá'u'lláh*

74

O Son of Man!
My eternity is My creation, I have created it for thee. Make it the garment of thy temple. My unity is My handiwork; I have wrought it for thee; clothe thyself therewith, that thou mayest be to all eternity the revelation of My everlasting being.

—*Bahá'u'lláh*

75

The essence of love is for man to turn his heart to the Beloved One, and sever himself from all else but Him, and desire naught save that which is the desire of his Lord.

—*Bahá'u'lláh*

76

I am, I am, I am the Promised One! I am the One Whose name you have for a thousand years invoked, at Whose mention you have risen, Whose advent you have longed to witness, and the hour of Whose Revelation you have prayed God to hasten. Verily, I say, it is incumbent upon the peoples of both the East and the West to obey My word, and to pledge allegiance to My person.

—*The Báb*

77

O ye peoples of the world! Know assuredly that My commandments are the lamps of My loving providence among My servants, and the keys of My mercy for My creatures. Thus hath it been sent down from the heaven of the Will of your Lord, the Lord of Revelation.

—*Bahá'u'lláh*

78

The first duty prescribed by God for His servants is the recognition of Him Who is the Dayspring of His Revelation and the Fountain of His laws, Who representeth the Godhead in both the Kingdom of His Cause and the world of creation. Whoso achieveth this duty hath attained unto all good; and whoso is deprived thereof hath gone astray, though he be the author of every righteous deed. It behooveth everyone who reacheth this most sublime station, this summit of transcendent glory, to observe every ordinance of Him Who is the Desire of the world. These twin duties are inseparable. Neither is acceptable without the other. Thus hath it been decreed by Him Who is the Source of Divine inspiration.

—*Bahá'u'lláh*

79

O Children of the Divine and Invisible Essence! Ye shall be hindered from loving Me and souls shall be perturbed as they make mention of Me. For minds cannot grasp Me nor hearts contain Me.

—*Bahá'u'lláh*

80

O Son of Spirit!
The time cometh, when the nightingale of holiness will no longer unfold the inner mysteries and ye will all be bereft of the celestial melody and of the voice from on high.

—*Bahá'u'lláh*

81

For the betterment of the world Bahá'u'lláh endured all the hardships, ordeals and vicissitudes of life, sacrificing His very being and comfort, forfeiting His estates, possessions and honor—all that pertains to human existence—not for one year, nay, rather, for nearly fifty years.

—*'Abdu'l-Bahá*

82

Let not your hearts be perturbed, O people, when the glory of My Presence is withdrawn, and the ocean of My utterance is stilled. In My presence amongst you there is a wisdom, and in My absence there is yet another, inscrutable to all but God, the Incomparable, the All-Knowing. Verily, We behold you from Our realm of glory, and shall aid whosoever will arise for the triumph of Our Cause with the hosts of the Concourse on high and a company of Our favored angels.

—*Bahá'u'lláh*

83

The Ancient Beauty [Bahá'u'lláh] hath consented to be bound with chains that mankind may be released from its bondage, and hath accepted to be made a prisoner within this most mighty Stronghold that the whole world may attain unto true liberty. He hath drained to its dregs the cup of sorrow, that all the peoples of the earth may attain unto abiding joy, and be filled with gladness.

—*Bahá'u'lláh*

84

Glorified be Thou, O my God! Behold Thou my head ready to fall before the sword of Thy Will, my neck prepared to bear the chains of Thy Desire, my heart yearning to be made a target for the darts of Thy Decree, mine eyes expectant to gaze on the tokens and signs of Thy wondrous Mercy.

—*Bahá'u'lláh*

85

Although Bahá'u'lláh was in prison the great Power of the Holy Spirit was with Him!

None other in prison could have been like unto Him. In spite of all the hardships He suffered, He never complained.

—*'Abdu'l-Bahá*

86

O Son of Man!
If adversity befall thee not in My path, how canst thou walk in the ways of them that are content with My pleasure? If trials afflict thee not in thy longing to meet Me, how wilt thou attain the light in thy love for My beauty?

—*Bahá'u'lláh*

87

O Son of Being!
Busy not thyself with this world, for with fire We test the gold, and with gold We test Our servants.

—*Bahá'u'lláh*

88

It behooveth him who expoundeth the Word of God to deliver it with the utmost goodwill, kindness, and compassion. As to him that embraceth the truth and is honored with recognizing Him, his name shall be recorded in the Crimson Book among the inmates of the all-highest Paradise. Should a soul fail, however, to accept the truth, it is in no wise permissible to contend with him. . . . In matters of religion every form of fanaticism, hatred, dissension and strife is strictly forbidden.

—*Bahá'u'lláh*

89

By My life and My Cause! Round about whatever dwelling the friends of God may enter, and from which their cry shall rise as they praise and glorify the Lord, shall circle the souls of true believers and all the favored angels. And should the door of the true eye be opened unto some, they shall witness the Supreme Concourse as it circleth and crieth: "Blessed art thou, O house, for God hath made thee a resting-place for those He favoreth, and a lodging for those He holdeth dear, and a home for those in whom He hath placed His trust. Unto thee be His praise and His glory and His endless grace."

—*Bahá'u'lláh*

90

All praise be to the one true God—exalted be His glory—inasmuch as He hath, through the Pen of the

Most High, unlocked the doors of men's hearts. Every verse which this Pen hath revealed is a bright and shining portal that discloseth the glories of a saintly and pious life, of pure and stainless deeds. The summons and the message which We gave were never intended to reach or to benefit one land or one people only. Mankind in its entirety must firmly adhere to whatsoever hath been revealed and vouchsafed unto it. Then and only then will it attain unto true liberty.

—*Bahá'u'lláh*

91

Immerse yourselves in the ocean of My words, that ye may unravel its secrets, and discover all the pearls of wisdom that lie hid in its depths. Take heed that ye do not vacillate in your determination to embrace the truth of this Cause—a Cause through which the potentialities of the might of God have been revealed, and His sovereignty established. With faces beaming with joy, hasten ye unto Him. This is the changeless Faith of God, eternal in the past, eternal in the future. Let him that seeketh, attain it; and as to him that hath refused to seek it—verily, God is Self-Sufficient, above any need of His creatures.

—*Bahá'u'lláh*

92

The Word of God is the king of words and its pervasive influence is incalculable. It hath ever dominated and will continue to dominate the realm of being. The Great Being saith: The Word is the master key for the whole world, inasmuch as through its potency the doors of the hearts of men, which in reality are the doors of heaven, are unlocked.

—*Bahá'u'lláh*

93

Act in such a way that your heart may be free from hatred. Let not your heart be offended with anyone. If some one commits an error and wrong toward you, you must instantly forgive him.

—*'Abdu'l-Bahá*

94

O Thou kind Lord! Thou hast created all humanity from the same stock. Thou hast decreed that all shall belong to the same household. In Thy Holy Presence they are all Thy servants, and all mankind are sheltered beneath Thy Tabernacle; all have gathered together at Thy Table of Bounty; all are illumined through the light of Thy Providence.

—*'Abdu'l-Bahá*

95

Praise be to the all-perceiving, the ever-abiding Lord Who, from a dewdrop out of the ocean of His grace, hath reared the firmament of existence, adorned it with the stars of knowledge, and admitted man into the lofty court of insight and understanding. This dewdrop, which is the Primal Word of God, is at times called the Water of Life, inasmuch as it quickeneth with the waters of knowledge them that have perished in the wilderness of ignorance.

—*Bahá'u'lláh*

96

Do thou meditate on that which We have revealed unto thee, that thou mayest discover the purpose of God, thy Lord, and the Lord of all worlds. In these words the mysteries of Divine Wisdom have been treasured.

—*Bahá'u'lláh*

97

Praise be to God, thy heart is engaged in the commemoration of God, thy soul is gladdened by the glad tidings of God and thou art absorbed in prayer. The state of prayer is the best of conditions, for man is then associating with God. Prayer verily bestoweth life, particularly when offered in private and at times, such as midnight, when freed from daily cares.

—*'Abdu'l-Bahá*

98

It behooveth the servant to pray to and seek assistance from God, and to supplicate and implore His aid. Such becometh the rank of servitude, and the Lord will decree whatsoever He desireth, in accordance with His consummate wisdom.

—*'Abdu'l-Bahá*

99

Bahá'u'lláh says there is a sign (from God) in every phenomenon: the sign of the intellect is contemplation and the sign of contemplation is silence, because it is impossible for a man to do two things at one time—he cannot both speak and meditate.

—*'Abdu'l-Bahá*

100

It is an axiomatic fact that while you meditate you are speaking with your own spirit. In that state of mind you put certain questions to your spirit and the spirit answers: the light breaks forth and the reality is revealed.

You cannot apply the name "man" to any being void of this faculty of meditation; without it he would be a mere animal, lower than the beasts.

Through the faculty of meditation man attains to eternal life; through it he receives the breath of the Holy Spirit—the bestowal of the Spirit is given in reflection and meditation.

The spirit of man is itself informed and strengthened during meditation; through it affairs of which man knew nothing are unfolded before his view. Through it he receives Divine inspiration, through it he receives heavenly food.

—*'Abdu'l-Bahá*

101

Beseech ye the one true God to grant that ye may taste the savor of such deeds as are performed in His path, and partake of the sweetness of such humility and submissiveness as are shown for His sake. Forget your own selves, and turn your eyes towards your neighbor. Bend your energies to whatever may foster the education of men. Nothing is, or can ever be, hidden from God. If ye follow in His way, His incalculable and imperishable blessings will be showered upon you. This is the luminous Tablet, whose verses have streamed from the moving Pen of Him Who is the Lord of all worlds. Ponder it in your hearts, and be ye of them that observe its precepts.

—*Bahá'u'lláh*

102

Every eye, in this Day, should seek what will best promote the Cause of God. He, Who is the Eternal Truth, beareth Me witness! Nothing whatever can, in this Day, inflict a greater harm upon this Cause than dissension and strife, contention, estrangement and apathy, among the loved ones of God. Flee them, through the power of God and His sovereign aid, and strive ye to knit together the hearts of men, in His Name, the Unifier, the All-Knowing, the All-Wise.

—*Bahá'u'lláh*

103

Every era hath a spirit; the spirit of this illumined era lieth in the teachings of Bahá'u'lláh. For these lay the foundation of the oneness of the world of humanity and promulgate universal brotherhood. They are founded upon the unity of science and religion and upon investigation of truth. They uphold the principle that religion must be the cause of amity, union and harmony among men. They establish the equality of both sexes and propound economic principles which are for the happiness of individuals. They diffuse universal education, that every soul may as much as possible have a share of knowledge. They abrogate and nullify religious, racial, political, patriotic and economic prejudices and the like. Those teachings that are scattered throughout the Epistles and Tablets are the cause of the illumination and the life of the world of humanity. Whoever promulgateth them will verily be assisted by the Kingdom of God.

—*'Abdu'l-Bahá*

104

I ask you all, each one of you, to follow well the light of truth, in the Holy Teachings, and God will strengthen you by His Holy Spirit so that you will be enabled to overcome the difficulties, and to destroy the prejudices which cause separation and hatred amongst the people. Let your hearts be filled with the great love of God, let it be felt by all; for every man is a servant of God, and all are entitled to a share of the Divine Bounty.

Especially to those whose thoughts are material and retrograde show the utmost love and patience, thereby winning them into the unity of fellowship by the radiance of your kindness.

—*'Abdu'l-Bahá*

105

O servant of God! We have bestowed a dewdrop from the ocean of divine grace; would that men might drink therefrom. We have brought a trace of the sweet melodies of the Beloved; would that men might hearken with their inner ear! Soar upon the wings of joy in the atmosphere of the love of God. Regard the people of the world as dead and seek the fellowship of the living. Whoso hath not breathed the sweet fragrance of the Beloved at this dawntide is indeed accounted among the dead. He Who is the All-Sufficing proclaimeth aloud: "The realm of joy hath been ushered in; be not sorrowful! The hidden mystery hath been made manifest; be not disheartened!" Wert thou to apprehend the surpassing greatness of this Day, thou wouldst renounce the world and all that dwell therein and hasten unto the way that leadeth to the Lord.

—*Bahá'u'lláh*

106

Consider the rational faculty with which God hath endowed the essence of man. Examine thine own self, and behold how thy motion and stillness, thy will and purpose, thy sight and hearing, thy sense of smell and power of speech, and whatever else is related to, or transcendeth, thy physical senses or spiritual perceptions, all proceed from, and owe their existence to, this same faculty. So closely are they related unto it, that if in less than the twinkling of an eye its relationship to the human body be severed, each and every one of these senses will cease immediately to exercise its function, and will be deprived of the power to manifest the evidences of its activity. It is indubitably clear and evident that each of these aforementioned instruments has depended, and will ever continue to depend, for its proper functioning on this rational faculty, which should be regarded as a sign of the revelation of Him Who is the sovereign Lord of all. Through its manifestation all these names and attributes have been revealed, and by the suspension of its action they are all destroyed and perish.

—*Bahá'u'lláh*

107

Know thou that God—exalted and glorified be He—doth in no wise manifest His inmost Essence and Reality. From time immemorial He hath been veiled in the eternity of His Essence and concealed in the infinitude of His own Being. And when He purposed to manifest His beauty in the kingdom of names and to reveal His glory in the realm of attributes, He brought forth His Prophets from the invisible plane to the visible, that His name "the Manifest" might be distinguished from "the Hidden" and His name "the Last" might be discerned from "the First," and that there may be fulfilled the words: "He is the First and the Last; the Seen and the Hidden; and He knoweth all things!" Thus hath He revealed these most excellent names and most exalted words in the Manifestations of His Self and the Mirrors of His Being.

—*Bahá'u'lláh*

108

You must love your friend better than yourself; yes, be willing to sacrifice yourself. . . . I desire that you be ready to sacrifice everything for each other, even life itself; then I will know that the Cause of Bahá'u'lláh has been established.

—*'Abdu'l-Bahá*

109

O Thou merciful God! O Thou Who art mighty and powerful! O Thou most kind Father! These servants have gathered together, turning to Thee, supplicating Thy threshold, desiring Thine endless bounties from Thy great assurance. They have no purpose save Thy good pleasure. They have no intention save service to the world of humanity.

—*'Abdu'l-Bahá*

110

The poor are especially beloved of God. Their lives are full of difficulties, their trials continual, their hopes are in God alone. Therefore, you must assist the poor as much as possible, even by sacrifice of yourself. No deed of man is greater before God than helping the poor. Spiritual conditions are not dependent upon the possession of worldly treasures or the absence of them. When one is physically destitute, spiritual thoughts are more likely. Poverty is a stimulus toward God. Each one of you must have great consideration for the poor and render them assistance. Organize in an effort to help them and prevent increase of poverty.

—*'Abdu'l-Bahá*

111

O My Servant!
Ye are the trees of My garden; ye must give forth goodly and wondrous fruits, that ye yourselves and others may profit therefrom. Thus it is incumbent on every one to engage in crafts and professions, for therein lies the secret of wealth, O men of understanding! For results depend upon means, and the grace of God shall be all-sufficient unto you. Trees that yield no fruit have been and will ever be for the fire.

—*Bahá'u'lláh*

112

Lay not on any soul a load which ye would not wish to be laid upon you, and desire not for any-one the things ye would not desire for yourselves. This is My best counsel unto you, did ye but observe it.

—*Bahá'u'lláh*

113

The fruits of the tree of man have ever been and are goodly deeds and a praiseworthy character.

—*Bahá'u'lláh*

114

I pray for you that you may be informed by the life of the Divine Spirit, so that you may be the means of educating others. The life and morals of a spiritual man are, in themselves, an education to those who know him.

—*'Abdu'l-Bahá*

115

In the world of existence there is no more powerful magnet than the magnet of love.

—*'Abdu'l-Bahá*

116

Faith is the magnet which draws the confirmation of the Merciful One. Service is the magnet which attracts the heavenly strength. I hope thou wilt attain both.

—*'Abdu'l-Bahá*

117

Teach unto your children the words that have been sent down from God, that they may recite them in the sweetest of tones. This standeth revealed in a mighty Book.

—*Bahá'u'lláh*

118

The beloved of God and the maid-servants of the Merciful must train their children with life and heart and teach them in the school of virtue and perfection.

—*'Abdu'l-Bahá*

119

As to thy question concerning training children: It is incumbent upon thee to nurture them from the breast of the love of God, to urge them towards spiritual matters, to turn unto God and to acquire good manners, best characteristics and praiseworthy virtues and qualities in the world of humanity, and to study sciences with the utmost diligence; so that they may become spiritual, heavenly and attracted to the fragrances of sanctity from their childhood and be reared in a religious, spiritual and heavenly training. Verily, I beg of God to confirm them therein.

—*'Abdu'l-Bahá*

120

The first trainer of the child is the mother. The babe, like unto a green and tender branch, will grow according to the way it is trained. If the training be right, it will grow right, and if crooked, the growth likewise, and unto the end of life it will conduct itself accordingly.

—*'Abdu'l-Bahá*

121

And among the teachings of Bahá'u'lláh is the equality of women and men. The world of humanity has two wings—one is women and the other men. Not until both wings are equally developed can the bird fly. Should one wing remain weak, flight is impossible. Not until the world of women becomes equal to the world of men in the acquisition of virtues and perfections, can success and prosperity be attained as they ought to be.

—*'Abdu'l-Bahá*

122

Women must endeavor to attain greater perfection, to be man's equal in every respect, to make progress in all in which she has been backward, so that man will be compelled to acknowledge her equality of capacity and attainment.

—*'Abdu'l-Bahá*

123

Delight not yourselves in the things of the world and its vain ornaments, neither set your hopes on them. Let your reliance be on the remembrance of God, the Most Exalted, the Most Great.

—*Bahá'u'lláh*

124

O people of God! Do not busy yourselves in your own concerns; let your thoughts be fixed upon that which will rehabilitate the fortunes of mankind and sanctify the hearts and souls of men. This can best be achieved through pure and holy deeds, through a virtuous life and a goodly behavior.

—*Bahá'u'lláh*

125

The light of a good character surpasseth the light of the sun and the radiance thereof. Whoso attaineth unto it is accounted as a jewel among men. The glory and upliftment of the world must needs depend upon it. A goodly character is a means whereby men are guided to the Straight Path.

—*Bahá'u'lláh*

126

The foundation of Bahá'u'lláh is love. . . . you must have infinite love for each other, each preferring the other before himself. The people must be so attracted to you that they will exclaim, "What happiness exists among you!" and will see in your faces the lights of the Kingdom; then in wonderment they will turn to you and seek the cause of your happiness.

—*'Abdu'l-Bahá*

127

[Self-love] is a strange trait and the means of the destruction of many important souls in the world. If man be imbued with all good qualities but be selfish, all the other virtues will fade or pass away and eventually he will grow worse.

—*'Abdu'l-Bahá*

128

Beware lest ye offend the feelings of anyone, or sadden the heart of any person, or move the tongue in reproach of and finding fault with anybody. . . .

—*'Abdu'l-Bahá*

129

O Ye Seeming Fair Yet Inwardly Foul!
Ye are like clear but bitter water, which to outward seeming is crystal pure but of which, when tested by the divine Assayer, not a drop is accepted. Yea, the sunbeam falls alike upon the dust and the mirror, yet differ they in reflection even as doth the star from the earth: nay, immeasurable is the difference!

—*Bahá'u'lláh*

130

Humility exalteth man to the heaven of glory and power, whilst pride abaseth him to the depths of wretchedness and degradation.

—*Bahá'u'lláh*

131

Fear not: I am come into this world to bear witness to the glory of sacrifice. . . . The drops of this consecrated blood will be the seed out of which will arise the mighty Tree of God, the Tree that will gather beneath its all-embracing shadow the peoples and kindreds of the earth.

—*The Báb*

132

Wert thou to attain to but a dewdrop of the crystal waters of divine knowledge, thou wouldst readily realize that true life is not the life of the flesh but the life of the spirit.

—*Bahá'u'lláh*

133

He [the true seeker] must never seek to exalt himself above anyone, must wash away from the tablet of his heart every trace of pride and vainglory, must cling unto patience and resignation, observe silence and refrain from idle talk. For the tongue is a smoldering fire, and excess of speech a deadly poison. Material fire consumeth the body, whereas the fire of the tongue devoureth both heart and soul.

—*Bahá'u'lláh*

134

O Son of Man!

Deny not My servant should he ask anything from thee, for his face is My face; be then abashed before Me.

—*Bahá'u'lláh*

135

Magnified be Thy name, O Lord my God! Thou art He Whom all things worship and Who worshipeth no one, Who is the Lord of all things and is the vassal of none, Who knoweth all things and is known of none. Thou didst wish to make Thyself known unto men; therefore Thou didst, through a word of Thy mouth, bring creation into being and fashion the universe. There is none other God except Thee, the Fashioner, the Creator, the Almighty, the Most Powerful.

—*Bahá'u'lláh*

136

The purpose of God in creating man hath been, and will ever be, to enable him to know his Creator and to attain His Presence. To this most excellent aim, this supreme objective, all the heavenly Books and the divinely revealed and weighty Scriptures unequivocally bear witness. Whoso hath recognized the Dayspring of Divine guidance and entered His holy court hath drawn nigh unto God and attained His Presence, a Presence which is the real Paradise. . . .

—*Bahá'u'lláh*

137

O Son of Man!

I loved thy creation, hence I created thee. Wherefore, do thou love Me, that I may name thy name and fill thy soul with the spirit of life.

—*Bahá'u'lláh*

138

Praise be unto God, incomparable in majesty, power and beauty, peerless in glory, might and grandeur; too high is He for human imaginations to comprehend Him or for any peer or equal to be ascribed unto Him.

—*Bahá'u'lláh*

139

O affectionate seeker! Shouldst thou soar in the holy realm of the spirit, thou wouldst recognize God manifest and exalted above all things, in such wise that thine eyes would behold none else but Him.

—*Bahá'u'lláh*

140

Between scientists and the followers of religion there has always been controversy and strife for the reason that the latter have proclaimed religion superior in authority to science and considered scientific announcement opposed to the teachings of religion. Bahá'u'lláh declared that religion is in complete harmony with science and reason. If religious belief and doctrine is at variance with reason, it proceeds from the limited mind of man and not from God; therefore, it is unworthy of belief and not deserving of attention; the heart finds no rest in it, and real faith is impossible. How can man believe that which he knows to be opposed to reason? . . . Reason is the first faculty of man, and the religion of God is in harmony with it. Bahá'u'lláh has removed this form of dissension and discord from among mankind and reconciled science with religion by revealing the pure teachings of the divine reality. This accomplishment is specialized to Him in this Day.

—*'Abdu'l-Bahá*

141

O My Friend in Word!
Ponder awhile. Hast thou ever heard that friend and foe should abide in one heart? Cast out then the stranger, that the Friend may enter His home.

—*Bahá'u'lláh*

142

O Son of Man!
Neglect not My commandments if thou lovest My beauty, and forget not My counsels if thou wouldst attain My good pleasure.

—*Bahá'u'lláh*

143

Religions are many, but the reality of religion is one. The days are many, but the sun is one. The fountains are many, but the fountainhead is one. The branches are many, but the tree is one.

The foundation of the divine religions is reality; were there no reality, there would be no religions. Abraham heralded reality. Moses promulgated reality. Christ established reality. Muḥammad was the Messenger of reality. The Báb was the door of reality. Bahá'u'lláh was the splendor of reality. Reality is one; it does not admit multiplicity or division. Reality is as the sun, which shines forth from different dawning points; it is as the light, which has illumined many lanterns.

Therefore, if the religions investigate reality and seek the essential truth of their own foundations, they will agree and no difference will be found.

—*'Abdu'l-Bahá*

144

The purpose of religion as revealed from the heaven of God's holy Will is to establish unity and concord amongst the peoples of the world; make it not the cause of dissension and strife. The religion of God and His divine law are the most potent instruments and the surest of all means for the dawning of the light of unity amongst men.

—*Bahá'u'lláh*

145

O My beloved friends! You are the bearers of the name of God in this Day. You have been chosen as the repositories of His mystery. It behooves each one of you to manifest the attributes of God, and to exemplify by your deed and words the signs of His righteousness, His power and glory. The very members of your body must bear witness to the loftiness of your purpose, the integrity of your life, the reality of your faith, and the exalted character of your devotion.

—*The Báb*

146

The essence of faith is fewness of words and abundance of deeds; he whose words exceed his deeds, know verily his death is better than his life.

—*Bahá'u'lláh*

147

The essence of religion is to testify unto that which the Lord hath revealed, and follow that which He hath ordained in His mighty Book.

—*Bahá'u'lláh*

148

The Prophets of God should be regarded as physicians whose task is to foster the well-being of the world and its peoples, that, through the spirit of oneness, they may heal the sickness of a divided humanity.

—*Bahá'u'lláh*

149

O Son of Man!

Should prosperity befall thee, rejoice not, and should abasement come upon thee, grieve not, for both shall pass away and be no more.

—*Bahá'u'lláh*

150

Entrance into the Kingdom is through the love of God, through detachment, through holiness and chastity, through truthfulness, purity, steadfastness, faithfulness and the sacrifice of life. . . .

For those who believe in God, who have love of God, and faith, life is excellent—that is, it is eternal; but to those souls who are veiled from God, although they have life, it is dark. . . .

—*'Abdu'l-Bahá*

151

Naught is seen in My temple but the Temple of God, and in My beauty but His Beauty, and in My being but His Being, and in My self but His Self, and in My movement but His Movement, and in My acquiescence but His Acquiescence, and in My pen but His Pen, the Mighty, the All-Praised. There hath not been in My soul but the Truth, and in Myself naught could be seen but God.

—*Bahá'u'lláh*

152

Were any of the all-embracing Manifestations of God to declare: "I am God," He, verily, speaketh the truth, and no doubt attacheth thereto. For it hath been repeatedly demonstrated that through their Revelation, their attributes and names, the Revelation of God, His names and His attributes, are made manifest in the world. . . . And were any of them to voice the utterance, "I am the Messenger of God," He, also, speaketh the truth, the indubitable truth.

—*Bahá'u'lláh*

153

Truthfulness is the foundation of all human virtues. Without truthfulness progress and success, in all of the worlds of God, are impossible for any soul. When this holy attribute is established in man, all the divine qualities will also be acquired.

—*'Abdu'l-Bahá*

154

We, verily, have chosen courtesy, and made it the true mark of such as are nigh unto Him. Courtesy is, in truth, a raiment which fitteth all men, whether young or old. Well is it with him that adorneth his temple therewith, and woe unto him who is deprived of this great bounty.

—*Bahá'u'lláh*

155

O Son of Spirit!
The best beloved of all things in My sight is Justice; turn not away therefrom if thou desirest Me, and neglect it not that I may confide in thee. By its aid thou shalt see with thine own eyes and not through the eyes of others, and shalt know of thine own knowledge and not through the knowledge of thy neighbor. Ponder this in thy heart; how it behooveth thee to be.

Verily justice is My gift to thee and the sign of My loving-kindness. Set it then before thine eyes.

—*Bahá'u'lláh*

156

The first teaching of Bahá'u'lláh is the duty incumbent upon all to investigate reality. What does it mean to investigate reality? It means that man must forget all hearsay and examine truth himself, for he does not know whether statements he hears are in accordance with reality or not.

—*'Abdu'l-Bahá*

157

God has given man the eye of investigation by which he may see and recognize truth. . . . Man is not intended to see through the eyes of another, hear through another's ears nor comprehend with another's brain. . . . Therefore, depend upon your own reason and judgment and adhere to the outcome of your own investigation. . . .

—*'Abdu'l-Bahá*

158

It is enjoined upon every one of you to engage in some form of occupation. . . . We have graciously exalted your engagement in such work to the rank of worship unto God, the True One. Ponder ye in your hearts the grace and the blessings of God and render thanks unto Him at eventide and at dawn.

—*Bahá'u'lláh*

159

O Ye That Pride Yourselves on Mortal Riches! Know ye in truth that wealth is a mighty barrier between the seeker and his desire, the lover and his beloved. The rich, but for a few, shall in no wise attain the court of His presence nor enter the city of content and resignation. Well is it then with him, who, being rich, is not hindered by his riches from the eternal kingdom, nor deprived by them of imperishable dominion.

—*Bahá'u'lláh*

160

The man who makes a piece of notepaper to the best of his ability, conscientiously, concentrating all his forces on perfecting it, is giving praise to God. Briefly, all effort and exertion put forth by man from the fullness of his heart is worship, if it is prompted by the highest motives and the will to do service to humanity.

—*'Abdu'l-Bahá*

161

That one indeed is a man who, today, dedicateth himself to the service of the entire human race.

—Bahá'u'lláh

162

O Son of My Handmaid!

Be not troubled in poverty nor confident in riches, for poverty is followed by riches, and riches are followed by poverty. Yet to be poor in all save God is a wondrous gift, belittle not the value thereof, for in the end it will make thee rich in God. . . .

—Bahá'u'lláh

163

Grief and sorrow do not come to us by chance, they are sent to us by the Divine Mercy for our own perfecting.

While a man is happy he may forget his God; but when grief comes and sorrows overwhelm him, then will he remember his Father Who is in Heaven, and Who is able to deliver him from his humiliations.

—'Abdu'l-Bahá

164

O Fleeting Shadow!

Pass beyond the baser stages of doubt and rise to the exalted heights of certainty. Open the eye of truth, that thou mayest behold the veilless Beauty and exclaim: Hallowed be the Lord, the most excellent of all creators!

—*Bahá'u'lláh*

165

Know, verily, that the soul is a sign of God, a heavenly gem whose reality the most learned of men hath failed to grasp, and whose mystery no mind, however acute, can ever hope to unravel. It is the first among all created things to declare the excellence of its Creator, the first to recognize His glory, to cleave to His truth, and to bow down in adoration before Him. If it be faithful to God, it will reflect His light, and will, eventually, return unto Him. If it fail, however, in its allegiance to its Creator, it will become a victim to self and passion, and will, in the end, sink in their depths.

—*Bahá'u'lláh*

166

O Son of Spirit!
There is no peace for thee save by renouncing thyself and turning unto Me; for it behooveth thee to glory in My name, not in thine own; to put thy trust in Me and not in thyself, since I desire to be loved alone and above all that is.

—*Bahá'u'lláh*

167

Entrance into the Kingdom is through the love of God, through detachment, through holiness and chastity, through truthfulness, purity, steadfastness, faithfulness, and the sacrifice of life.

—*'Abdu'l-Bahá*

168

O Son of Light!
Forget all save Me and commune with My spirit. This is of the essence of My command, therefore turn unto it.

—*Bahá'u'lláh*

169

The wisdom of prayer is this: That it causeth a connection between the servant and the True One, because in that state man with all heart and soul turneth his face towards His Highness the Almighty, seeking His association and desiring His love and compassion.

—*'Abdu'l-Bahá*

170

Consider to what extent the love of God makes itself manifest. Among the signs of His love which appear in the world are the dawning points of His Manifestations. What an infinite degree of love is reflected by the divine Manifestations toward mankind! For the sake of guiding the people They have willingly forfeited Their lives to resuscitate human hearts. . . .

Observe how rarely human souls sacrifice their pleasure or comfort for others, how improbable that a man would offer his eye or suffer himself to be dismembered for the benefit of another. Yet all the divine Manifestations suffered, offered Their lives and blood, sacrificed Their existence, comfort and all They possessed for the sake of mankind. Therefore, consider how much They love. Were it not for Their love for humanity, spiritual love would be mere nomenclature. Were it not for Their illumination, human souls would not be radiant. How effective is Their love! This is a sign of the love of God, a ray of the Sun of Reality.

—*'Abdu'l-Bahá*

171

Each one must sacrifice his life and possessions to the other and each person be loving to all the inhabitants of the world, rending asunder the curtain of foreignness and consorting with all the people with union and accord.

—*'Abdu'l-Bahá*

172

To attain eternal happiness one must suffer. He who has reached the state of self-sacrifice has true joy. Temporal joy will vanish.

—*'Abdu'l-Bahá*

173

O Son of Spirit!
Vaunt not thyself over the poor, for I lead him on his way and behold thee in thy evil plight and confound thee for evermore.

—*Bahá'u'lláh*

174

O Son of Passion!
Cleanse thyself from the defilement of riches and in perfect peace advance into the realm of poverty; that from the wellspring of detachment thou mayest quaff the wine of immortal life.

—*Bahá'u'lláh*

175

O Son of Beauty!
By My spirit and by My favor! By My mercy and by My beauty! All that I have revealed unto thee with the tongue of power, and have written for thee with the pen of might, hath been in accordance with thy

capacity and understanding, not with My state and the melody of My voice.

—*Bahá'u'lláh*

176

Pride not yourselves on much reading of the verses or on a multitude of pious acts by night and day; for were a man to read a single verse with joy and radiance it would be better for him than to read with lassitude all the Holy Books of God, the Help in Peril, the Self-Subsisting. Read ye the sacred verses in such measure that ye be not overcome by languor and despondency. Lay not upon your souls that which will weary them and weigh them down, but rather what will lighten and uplift them, so that they may soar on the wings of the Divine verses towards the Dawning-place of His manifest signs; this will draw you nearer to God, did ye but comprehend.

—*Bahá'u'lláh*

177

O God! Thou art kind to all, Thou hast provided for all, dost shelter all, conferrest life upon all. Thou hast endowed each and all with talents and faculties, and all are submerged in the Ocean of Thy Mercy.

O Thou kind Lord! Unite all. Let the religions agree and make the nations one, so that they may see each other as one family and the whole earth as one home. May they all live together in perfect harmony.

—*'Abdu'l-Bahá*

178

Heed not your weaknesses and frailty; fix your gaze upon the invincible power of the Lord, your God, the Almighty. . . . Arise in His name, put your trust wholly in Him, and be assured of ultimate victory.

—*The Báb*

179

Lift up your hearts above the present and look with eyes of faith into the future! Today the seed is sown, the grain falls upon the earth, but behold the day will come when it shall rise a glorious tree and the branches thereof shall be laden with fruit.

—*'Abdu'l-Bahá*

180

O Son of Being!
Seek a martyr's death in My path, content with My pleasure and thankful for that which I ordain, that thou mayest repose with Me beneath the canopy of majesty behind the tabernacle of glory.

—*Bahá'u'lláh*

181

This earthly life shall come to an end, and everyone shall expire and return unto my Lord God Who will reward with the choicest gifts the deeds of those who endure with patience.

—*The Báb*

182

O Son of Man!
Ponder and reflect. Is it thy wish to die upon thy bed, or to shed thy lifeblood on the dust, a martyr in My path, and so become the manifestation of My command and the revealer of My light in the highest paradise? Judge thou aright, O servant!

—*Bahá'u'lláh*

183

O my Lord! Make Thy beauty to be my food, and Thy presence my drink, and Thy pleasure my hope, and praise of Thee my action, and remembrance of Thee my companion, and the power of Thy sovereignty my succorer, and Thy habitation my home, and my dwelling-place the seat Thou hast sanctified from the limitations imposed upon them who are shut out as by a veil from Thee.

—*Bahá'u'lláh*

184

I have no will but Thy will, O my Lord, and cherish no desire except Thy desire. From my pen floweth only the summons which Thine own exalted pen hath voiced, and my tongue uttereth naught save what the Most Great Spirit hath itself proclaimed in the kingdom of Thine eternity.

—*Bahá'u'lláh*

185

We have revealed in Our Most Holy Book: "When the ocean of My presence hath ebbed and the Book of My Revelation is ended, turn your faces toward Him Whom God hath purposed, Who hath branched from this Ancient Root." The object of this sacred verse is none other except the Most Mighty Branch ['Abdu'l-Bahá]. Thus have We graciously revealed unto you our potent Will, and I am verily the Gracious, the All-Powerful.

—*Bahá'u'lláh*

186

Humanity is not perfect. There are imperfections in every human being, and you will always become unhappy if you look toward the people themselves. But if you look toward God, you will love them and be kind to them, for the world of God is the world of perfection and complete mercy.

—*'Abdu'l-Bahá*

187

It is indeed a good and praiseworthy thing to progress materially, but in so doing, let us not neglect the more important spiritual progress, and close our eyes to the Divine light shining in our midst.

—*'Abdu'l-Bahá*

188

Man has the power both to do good and to do evil; if his power for good predominates and his inclinations to do wrong are conquered, then man in truth may be called a saint.

—*'Abdu'l-Bahá*

189

The knowledge of the Reality of the Divinity is impossible and unattainable, but the knowledge of the Manifestations of God is the knowledge of God, for the bounties, splendors, and divine attributes are apparent in Them.

—*'Abdu'l-Bahá*

190

The diversity in the human family should be the cause of love and harmony, as it is in music where many different notes blend together in the making of a perfect chord.

—*'Abdu'l-Bahá*

191

When you meet those whose opinions differ from your own, do not turn away your face from them. All are seeking truth, and there are many roads leading thereto. Truth has many aspects, but it remains always and forever one.

Do not allow difference of opinion, or diversity of thought to separate you from your fellowmen, or to be the cause of dispute, hatred and strife in your hearts.

Rather, search diligently for the truth and make all men your friends.

—*'Abdu'l-Bahá*

192

What a power is love! It is the most wonderful, the greatest of all living powers.

Love gives life to the lifeless. Love lights a flame in the heart that is cold. Love brings hope to the hopeless and gladdens the hearts of the sorrowful.

In the world of existence there is indeed no greater power than the power of love.

—*'Abdu'l-Bahá*

193

The world's equilibrium hath been upset through the vibrating influence of this most great, this new World Order. Mankind's ordered life hath been revolutionized through the agency of this unique, this wondrous System—the like of which mortal eyes have never witnessed.

—*Bahá'u'lláh*

194

I am but a poor creature, O my Lord; I have clung to the hem of Thy riches. I am sore sick; I have held fast the cord of Thy healing. Deliver me from the ills that have encircled me, and wash me thoroughly with the waters of Thy graciousness and mercy. . . .

—*Bahá'u'lláh*

195

If ye become aware of a sin committed by another, conceal it, that God may conceal your own sin. He, verily, is the Concealer, the Lord of grace abounding.

—*Bahá'u'lláh*

196

That which ye were promised in the Kingdom of God is fulfilled. This is the Word which the Son veiled when He said to those around Him that at that time they could not bear it . . .Verily the Spirit of Truth is come to guide you unto all truth . . . He is the One Who glorified the Son and exalted His Cause.

—*Bahá'u'lláh*

197

The time foreordained unto the peoples and kindreds of the earth is now come. The promises of God, as recorded in the holy Scriptures, have all been fulfilled.

—*Bahá'u'lláh*

198

The day is approaching when the wrathful anger of the Almighty will have taken hold of them. . . . He shall cleanse the earth from the defilement of their corruption, and shall give it for an heritage unto such of His servants as are nigh unto Him.

—*Bahá'u'lláh*

199

The body of the human world is sick. Its remedy and healing will be the oneness of the kingdom of humanity. Its life is the Most Great Peace. Its illumination and quickening is love. Its happiness is the attainment of spiritual perfections.

—*'Abdu'l-Bahá*

200

Today there is no greater glory for man than that of service in the cause of the Most Great Peace. Peace is light, whereas war is darkness. Peace is life; war is death. Peace is guidance; war is error. Peace is the foundation of God; war is a satanic institution. Peace is the illumination of the world of humanity; war is the destroyer of human foundations.

—*'Abdu'l-Bahá*

201

May you become as the waves of one sea, stars of the same heaven, fruits adorning the same tree, roses of one garden in order that through you the oneness of humanity may establish its temple in the world of mankind, for you are the ones who are called to uplift the cause of unity among the nations of the earth.

—*'Abdu'l-Bahá*

202

Love and unity are the needs of the body politic today. Without these there can be no progress or prosperity attained. Therefore, the friends of God must adhere to the power which will create this love and unity in the hearts of the sons of men.

—*'Abdu'l-Bahá*

203

I charge you all that each one of you concentrate all the thoughts of your heart on love and unity. When a thought of war comes, oppose it by a stronger thought of peace. A thought of hatred must be destroyed by a more powerful thought of love.

—*'Abdu'l-Bahá*

204

O servant of God! The day of deeds hath come: Now is not the time for words. The Messenger of God hath appeared: Now is not the hour for hesitation. Open thou thine inner eye that thou mayest behold the face of the Beloved, and hearken thou with thine inner ear that thou mayest hear the sweet murmur of His celestial voice.

—*Bahá'u'lláh*

205

O servants! If your heart acheth for the Beloved, lo, the remedy is come! If ye have eyes to see, behold, the shining countenance of the Friend hath appeared! Kindle ye the fire of knowledge and flee from the ignorant. Such are the words of the Lord of the world.

—*Bahá'u'lláh*

206

O Servants! Verily I say, he is to be accounted as truthful who hath beheld the straight Path. That Path is one, and God hath chosen and prepared it. It shineth resplendent amongst all paths as the sun amongst the stars. Whosoever hath not attained it hath failed to apprehend the truth and hath gone astray. Such are the counsels of the incomparable, the peerless Lord.

—*Bahá'u'lláh*

207

O servants! Ye are even as saplings in a garden, which are near to perishing for want of water. Wherefore, revive your souls with the heavenly water that is raining down from the clouds of divine bounty.

—*Bahá'u'lláh*

208

Anguish and torment, when suffered on the pathway of the Lord, Him of manifest signs, is only favor and grace; affliction is but mercy, and grief a gift from God. Poison is sugar on the tongue, and wrath is kindness, nourishing the soul.

—*'Abdu'l-Bahá*

209

Not every mortal frame hath a spirit or is imbued with life. In this day he is endowed with spirit who with all his heart seeketh the abode of the Beloved. The end of all beginnings is to be found in this Day: Turn ye not a blind eye unto it. The matchless Friend is nigh: Stray not far from Him.

—*Bahá'u'lláh*

210

The fleeting hours of man's life on earth pass swiftly by and the little that still remaineth shall come to an end, but that which endureth and lasteth for evermore is the fruit that man reapeth from his servitude at the Divine Threshold. Behold the truth of this saying, how abundant and glorious are the proofs thereof in the world of being!

—*'Abdu'l-Bahá*

211

The essence of Bahá'u'lláh's Teaching is all-embracing love, for love includeth every excellence of humankind. It causeth every soul to go forward. It bestoweth on each one, for a heritage, immortal life. Erelong shalt thou bear witness that His celestial Teachings, the very glory of reality itself, shall light up the skies of the world.

—*'Abdu'l-Bahá*

212

The great and fundamental teachings of Bahá'u'lláh are the oneness of God and unity of mankind. This is the bond of union among Bahá'ís all over the world. They become united themselves, then unite others. It is impossible to unite unless united.

—*'Abdu'l-Bahá*

213

O thou seeker after the Kingdom! Every divine Manifestation is the very life of the world, and the skilled physician of each ailing soul. The world of man is sick, and that competent Physician knoweth the cure, arising as He doth with teachings, counsels and admonishments that are the remedy for every pain, the healing balm to every wound. It is certain that the wise physician can diagnose his patient's needs at any season, and apply the cure. Wherefore, relate thou the Teachings of the Abhá Beauty* to the urgent needs of this present day, and thou wilt see that they provide an instant remedy for the ailing body of the world. Indeed, they are the elixir that bringeth eternal health.

—*'Abdu'l-Bahá*

214

So powerful is the light of unity that it can illuminate the whole earth. The one true God, He Who knoweth all things, Himself testifieth to the truth of these words. . . . This goal excelleth every other goal, and this aspiration is the monarch of all aspirations.

—*Bahá'u'lláh*

215

He Who is your Lord, the All-Merciful, cherisheth in His heart the desire of beholding the entire human race as one soul and one body. Haste ye to win your share of God's good grace and mercy in this Day that eclipseth all other created days.

—*Bahá'u'lláh*

* Bahá'u'lláh.

216

All nations and kindreds will be gathered together under the shadow of this Divine Banner . . . and will become a single nation. Religious and sectarian antagonism, the hostility of races and peoples, and differences among nations, will be eliminated. All men will adhere to one religion, will have one common faith, will be blended into one race and become a single people. All will dwell in one common fatherland, which is the planet itself.

—'Abdu'l-Bahá

217

The fear of God hath ever been a sure defense and a safe stronghold for all the peoples of the world. It is the chief cause of the protection of mankind, and the supreme instrument for its preservation. Indeed, there existeth in man a faculty which deterreth him from, and guardeth him against, whatever is unworthy and unseemly, and which is known as his sense of shame. This, however, is confined to but a few; all have not possessed, and do not possess, it.

—Bahá'u'lláh

218

Every Prophet Whom the Almighty and Peerless Creator hath purposed to send to the peoples of the earth hath been entrusted with a Message, and charged to act in a manner that would best meet the requirements of the age in which He appeared.

—*Bahá'u'lláh*

219

God leaves not His children comfortless, but, when the darkness of winter overshadows them, then again He sends His Messengers, the Prophets, with a renewal of the blessed spring.

—*'Abdu'l-Bahá*

220

The Heavenly Books, the Bible, the Qur'án, and the other Holy Writings have been given by God as guides into the paths of Divine virtue, love, justice and peace.

—*'Abdu'l-Bahá*

221

The message of Krishna is the message of love. All God's prophets have brought the message of love.

—*'Abdu'l-Bahá*

222

The essence of faith is fewness of words and abundance of deeds.

—*Bahá'u'lláh*

223

That seeker must at all times put his trust in God, must renounce the peoples of the earth, detach himself from the world of dust, and cleave unto Him Who is the Lord of Lords.

—*Bahá'u'lláh*

224

The Prophets of God should be regarded as physicians whose task is to foster the well-being of the world and its peoples, that, through the spirit of oneness, they may heal the sickness of a divided humanity.

—*Bahá'u'lláh*

225

O Son of Man!
Thou dost wish for gold and I desire thy freedom from it. Thou thinkest thyself rich in its possession, and I recognize thy wealth in thy sanctity therefrom. By My life! This is My knowledge, and that is thy fancy; how can My way accord with thine?

—*Bahá'u'lláh*

226

Man's glory lieth in his knowledge, his upright conduct, his praiseworthy character, his wisdom, and not in his nationality or rank.

—*Bahá'u'lláh*

227

O Son of Man!

Breathe not the sins of others so long as thou art thyself a sinner. Shouldst thou transgress this command, accursed wouldst thou be, and to this I bear witness.

—*Bahá'u'lláh*

228

A kindly tongue is the lodestone of the hearts of men. It is the bread of the spirit, it clotheth the words with meaning, it is the fountain of the light of wisdom and understanding. . . .

—*Bahá'u'lláh*

229

O Son of Being!

Love Me, that I may love thee. If thou lovest Me not, My love can in no wise reach thee. Know this, O servant.

—*Bahá'u'lláh*

230

To the blind Thou hast given sight; to the deaf Thou hast granted hearing; Thou hast resuscitated the dead; Thou hast enriched the poor. . . .

—*'Abdu'l-Bahá*

231

The Divine Reality may be likened to the sun and the Holy Spirit to the rays of the sun. As the rays of the sun bring the light and warmth of the sun to the earth, giving life to all created beings, so do the "Manifestations" [of God] bring the power of the Holy Spirit from the Divine Sun of Reality to give light and life to the souls of men.

—*'Abdu'l-Bahá*

232

Moses and the Mosaic law were the unifying center for the scattered sheep of Israel. He united these wandering flocks, brought them under control of divine law, educated and unified them, caused them to agree and uplifted them to a superlative degree of development.

—*'Abdu'l-Bahá*

233

It is a basic principle of the Law of God that in every Prophetic Mission, He entereth into a Covenant with all believers—a Covenant that endureth until the end of that Mission. . . . Consider Moses, He Who conversed with God. Verily, upon Mount Sinai, Moses entered into a Covenant regarding the Messiah, with all those souls who would live in the day of the Messiah. And those souls, although they appeared many centuries after Moses, were nevertheless—so far as the Covenant, which is outside time, was concerned—present there with Moses. The Jews, however, were heedless of this and remembered it not, and thus they suffered a great and clear loss.

—'Abdu'l-Bahá

234

The essence of wealth is love for Me; whoso loveth Me is the possessor of all things, and he that loveth Me not is indeed of the poor and needy. This is that which the Finger of Glory and Splendor hath revealed.

—Bahá'u'lláh

235

Fear thou God and pride not thyself on thine earthly possessions, inasmuch as what God doth possess is better for them that tread the path of righteousness.

— The Báb

236

O God! Refresh and gladden my spirit. Purify my heart. Illumine my powers. I lay all my affairs in Thy hand. Thou art my Guide and my Refuge.

—'Abdu'l-Bahá

237

O Son of Man!
Be thou content with Me and seek no other helper. For none but Me can ever suffice thee.

—*Bahá'u'lláh*

238

Knowledge is love. Study, listen to exhortations, think, try to understand the wisdom and greatness of God. The soil must be fertilized before the seed can be sown.

—*'Abdu'l-Bahá*

239

In truth, knowledge is a veritable treasure for man, and a source of glory, of bounty, of joy, of exaltation, of cheer and gladness unto him.

—*Bahá'u'lláh*

240

The greatest bestowal of God in the world of humanity is religion, for assuredly the divine teachings of religion are above all other sources of instruction and development to man.

—*'Abdu'l-Bahá*

241

That which the Lord hath ordained as the sovereign remedy and mightiest instrument for the healing of all the world is the union of all its peoples in one universal Cause, one common Faith. This can in no wise be achieved except through the power of a skilled, an all-powerful and inspired Physician.

—*Bahá'u'lláh*

242

Concerning the prejudice of race: it is an illusion, a superstition pure and simple! For God created us all of one race.

—*'Abdu'l-Bahá*

243

Is there any Remover of difficulties save God? Say: Praised be God! He is God! All are His servants, and all abide by His bidding!

— *The Báb*

244

The holy Manifestations Who have been the Sources or Founders of the various religious systems were united and agreed in purpose and teaching. Abraham,

Moses, Zoroaster, Buddha, Jesus, Muḥammad, the Báb and Bahá'u'lláh are one in spirit and reality. Moreover, each Prophet fulfilled the promise of the One Who came before Him and, likewise, Each announced the One Who would follow.

—*'Abdu'l-Bahá*

245

The Person of the Manifestation hath ever been the representative and mouthpiece of God. He, in truth, is the Dayspring of God's most excellent Titles, and the Dawning-Place of His exalted Attributes.

—*Bahá'u'lláh*

246

The Word which the Son concealed is made manifest. It hath been sent down in the form of the human temple in this day.

—*Bahá'u'lláh*

247

There can be no doubt whatever that the peoples of the world, of whatever race or religion, derive their inspiration from one heavenly Source, and are the subjects of one God.

—*Bahá'u'lláh*

248

Be ye compassionate and kind to all the human race. Deal ye with strangers the same as with friends, cherish ye others just as ye would your own. See foes as friends; see demons as angels; give to the tyrant the same great love ye show the loyal and true. . . .

—*'Abdu'l-Bahá*

249

Know thou assuredly that the essence of all the Prophets of God is one and the same. Their unity is absolute. God, the Creator, saith: There is no distinction whatsoever among the Bearers of My Message.

—*Bahá'u'lláh*

250

Each Prophet fulfilled the promise of the One Who came before Him and, likewise, Each announced the One Who would follow. Consider how Abraham foretold the coming of Moses, and Moses embodied the Abrahamic statement. Moses prophesied the Messianic cycle, and Christ fulfilled the law of Moses. It is evident, therefore, that the Holy Manifestations Who founded the religious systems are united and agreed; there is no differentiation possible in Their mission and teachings; all are reflectors of reality, and all are promulgators of the religion of God. The divine religion is reality, and reality is not multiple; it is one. Therefore, the foundations of the religious systems are one because all proceed from the indivisible reality.

—*'Abdu'l-Bahá*

251

Know thou . . . that . . . women are accounted the same as men, and God hath created all humankind in His own image, and after His own likeness. That is, men and women alike are the revealers of His names and attributes, and from the spiritual viewpoint there is no difference between them. Whosoever draweth nearer to God, that one is the most favored, whether man or woman.

—*'Abdu'l-Bahá*

252

Let it be known . . . that until woman and man recognize and realize equality, social and political progress here or anywhere will not be possible. For the world of humanity consists of two parts or members: one is woman; the other is man. Until these two members are equal in strength, the oneness of humanity cannot be established, and the happiness and felicity of mankind will not be a reality.

—*'Abdu'l-Bahá*

253

Remembrance of God is like the rain and dew which bestow freshness and grace on flowers and hyacinths, revive them and cause them to acquire fragrance, redolence and renewed charm. . . . Strive thou, then, to praise and glorify God by night and by day, that thou mayest attain infinite freshness and beauty.

—*'Abdu'l-Bahá*

254

The publication of high thoughts is the dynamic power in the arteries of life; it is the very soul of the world. Thoughts are a boundless sea, and the effects and varying conditions of existence are as the separate forms and individual limits of the waves; not until the sea boils up will the waves rise and scatter their pearls of knowledge on the shore of life.

—*'Abdu'l-Bahá*

255

By the righteousness of God! Whoso openeth his lips in this Day and maketh mention of the name of his

Lord, the hosts of Divine inspiration shall descend upon him from the heaven of My name, the All-Knowing, the All-Wise. On him shall also descend the Concourse on high, each bearing aloft a chalice of pure light. Thus hath it been foreordained in the realm of God's Revelation, by the behest of Him Who is the All-Glorious, the Most Powerful.

—*Bahá'u'lláh*

256

They whom God hath endued with insight will readily recognize that the precepts laid down by God constitute the highest means for the maintenance of order in the world and the security of its peoples.

—*Bahá'u'lláh*

257

Religion is the light of the world, and the progress, achievement, and happiness of man result from obedience to the laws set down in the holy Books.

—*'Abdu'l-Bahá*

258

O ye children of men! The fundamental purpose animating the Faith of God and His Religion is to safeguard the interests and promote the unity of the human race, and to foster the spirit of love and fellowship amongst men.

—Bahá'u'lláh

259

Great is the blessedness of him who hath in this Day cast away the things current amongst men and hath clung unto that which is ordained by God, the Lord of Names and the Fashioner of all created things, He Who is come from the heaven of eternity through the power of the Most Great Name, invested with so invincible an authority that all the powers of the earth are unable to withstand Him. Unto this beareth witness the Mother Book, calling from the Most Sublime Station.

—Bahá'u'lláh

260

O Lord! Unite and bind together the hearts, join in accord all the souls, and exhilarate the spirits through the signs of Thy sanctity and oneness. O Lord! Make these faces radiant through the light of Thy oneness. Strengthen the loins of Thy servants in the service of Thy kingdom.

—'Abdu'l-Bahá

261

O Children of Men!
Know ye not why We created you all from the same dust? That no one should exalt himself over the other.

—Bahá'u'lláh

262

The unity which is productive of unlimited results is first a unity of mankind which recognizes that all are sheltered beneath the overshadowing glory of the All-Glorious, that all are servants of one God; for all breathe the same atmosphere, live upon the same earth, move beneath the same heavens, receive effulgence from the same sun and are under the protection of one God.

—'Abdu'l-Bahá

263

Recognize your enemies as friends, and consider those who wish you evil as the wishers of good.

—'Abdu'l-Bahá

264

O my God! O my God! Unite the hearts of Thy servants, and reveal to them Thy great purpose. May they follow Thy commandments and abide in Thy law. Help them, O God, in their endeavor, and grant them strength to serve Thee. O God! Leave them not to themselves, but guide their steps by the light of Thy knowledge, and cheer their hearts by Thy love. Verily, Thou art their Helper and their Lord.

—*Bahá'u'lláh*

265

It is not for him to pride himself who loveth his own country, but rather for him who loveth the whole world. The earth is but one country, and mankind its citizens.

—*Bahá'u'lláh*

266

The whole world must be looked upon as one single country, all the nations as one nation, all men as belonging to one race.

—*'Abdu'l-Bahá*

267

Do not be satisfied until each one with whom you are concerned is to you as a member of your family. Regard each one either as a father, or as a brother, or as a sister, or as a mother, or as a child. If you can attain to this, your difficulties will vanish, you will know what to do.

—*'Abdu'l-Bahá*

268

He is supreme over His servants, and standeth over His creatures. In His hand is the source of authority and truth. He maketh men alive by His signs, and causeth them to die through His wrath. He shall not be asked of His doings and His might is equal unto all things.

—Bahá'u'lláh

269

Address yourselves to the promotion of the well-being and tranquility of the children of men. Bend your minds and wills to the education of the peoples and kindreds of the earth, that haply the dissensions that divide it may, through the power of the Most Great Name, be blotted out from its face, and all mankind become the upholders of one Order, and the inhabitants of one City. Illumine and hallow your hearts; let them not be profaned by the thorns of hate or the thistles of malice. Ye dwell in one world, and have been created through the operation of one Will. Blessed is he who mingleth with all men in a spirit of utmost kindliness and love.

—Bahá'u'lláh

270

Know that in every home where God is praised and prayed to, and His Kingdom proclaimed, that home is a garden of God and a paradise of His happiness.

—*'Abdu'l-Bahá*

271

If love and agreement are manifest in a single family, that family will advance, become illumined and spiritual; but if enmity and hatred exist within it, destruction and dispersion are inevitable.

—*'Abdu'l-Bahá*

272

According to the teachings of Bahá'u'lláh the family, being a human unit, must be educated according to the rules of sanctity. All the virtues must be taught the family. The integrity of the family bond must be constantly considered, and the rights of the individual members must not be transgressed. The rights of the son, the father, the mother—none of them must be transgressed, none of them must be arbitrary. Just as the son has certain obligations to his father, the father, likewise, has certain obligations to his son. The mother, the sister and other members of the household have their certain prerogatives. All these rights and prerogatives must be conserved, yet the unity of the family must be sustained. The injury of one shall be considered the injury of all; the comfort of each, the comfort of all; the honor of one, the honor of all.

—*'Abdu'l-Bahá*

273

Concerning the prejudice of race: it is an illusion, a superstition pure and simple! For God created us all of one race. There were no differences in the beginning, for we are all descendants of Adam. In the beginning, also, there were no limits and boundaries between the different lands; no part of the earth belonged more to one people than to another.

—*'Abdu'l-Bahá*

274

In the world of being, the meeting is blessed when the white and colored races meet together with infinite spiritual love and heavenly harmony. When such meetings are established, and the participants associate with each other with perfect love, unity and kindness, the angels of the Kingdom praise them, and the Beauty of Bahá'u'lláh addresseth them, "Blessed are ye! Blessed are ye!"

—*'Abdu'l-Bahá*

275

There are no whites and blacks before God. All colors are one, and that is the color of servitude to God. Scent and color are not important. The heart is important. If the heart is pure, white or black or any color makes no difference. God does not look at colors; He looks at the hearts. He whose heart is pure is better. He whose character is better is more pleasing.

—*'Abdu'l-Bahá*

276

Arts, crafts and sciences uplift the world of being, and are conducive to its exaltation. Knowledge is as wings to man's life, and a ladder for his ascent. Its acquisition is incumbent upon everyone. The knowledge of such sciences, however, should be acquired as can profit the peoples of the earth, and not those which begin with words and end with words.

—*Bahá'u'lláh*

277

The flame of the fire of love, in this world of earth and water, comes through the power of attraction and not by effort and striving. Nevertheless, by effort and perseverance, knowledge, science and other perfections can be acquired; but only the light of the Divine Beauty can transport and move the spirits through the force of attraction. Therefore, it is said: "Many are called, but few are chosen."

—*'Abdu'l-Bahá*

278

Put all your beliefs into harmony with science; there can be no opposition, for truth is one. When religion, shorn of its superstitions, traditions, and unintelligent dogmas, shows its conformity with science, then will there be a great unifying, cleansing force in the world which will sweep before it all wars, disagreements, discords and struggles—and then will mankind be united in the power of the Love of God.

—*'Abdu'l-Bahá*

279

Religion must stand the analysis of reason. It must agree with scientific fact and proof so that science will sanction religion and religion fortify science. Both are indissolubly welded and joined in reality.

—*'Abdu'l-Bahá*

280

Religion must be in harmony with science and reason. If it does not conform to science and reconcile with reason, it is superstition.

—*'Abdu'l-Bahá*

281

Every time I lift up mine eyes unto Thy heaven, I call to mind Thy highness and Thy loftiness, and Thine incomparable glory and greatness; and every time I turn my gaze to Thine earth, I am made to recognize the evidences of Thy power and the tokens of Thy bounty.

—*Bahá'u'lláh*

282

This is a new cycle of human power. All the horizons of the world are luminous, and the world will become indeed as a garden and a paradise. . . . You are loosed from ancient superstitions which have kept men ignorant, destroying the foundation of true humanity.

The gift of God to this enlightened age is the knowledge of the oneness of mankind and of the fundamental oneness of religion. War shall cease between nations, and by the will of God the Most Great Peace shall come; the world will be seen as a new world, and all men will live as brothers.

—*'Abdu'l-Bahá*

283

Heedless souls are always seeking faults in others. What can the hypocrite know of others' faults when he is blind to his own? . . . As long as man does not find his own faults, he can never become perfect. Nothing is more fruitful for man than the knowledge of his own shortcomings.

—'Abdu'l-Bahá

284

God will answer the prayer of every servant if that prayer is urgent. His mercy is vast, illimitable. He answers the prayers of all His servants. . . .

. . . we ask for things which the divine wisdom does not desire for us, and there is no answer to our prayer. His wisdom does not sanction what we wish. . . . But whatever we ask for which is in accord with divine wisdom, God will answer. Assuredly! . . .

—'Abdu'l-Bahá

285

Oh, trust in God! for His Bounty is everlasting, and in His Blessings, for they are superb. Oh! put your faith in the Almighty, for He faileth not and His goodness endureth forever! His Sun giveth Light continually, and the Clouds of His Mercy are full of the Waters of Compassion with which He waters the hearts of all who trust in Him. His refreshing Breeze ever carries healing in its wings to the parched souls of men!

—'Abdu'l-Bahá

286

Bahá'u'lláh has written a Covenant and Testament with His own pen, declaring that the One Whom He has appointed the Center of the Covenant shall be turned to and obeyed by all. Therefore, thank God that Bahá'u'lláh has made the pathway straight. He has clearly explained all things and opened every door for advancing souls. There is no reason for hesitation by anyone. The purpose of the Covenant was simply to ward off disunion and differences so that no one might say, "My opinion is the true and valid one."

—*'Abdu'l-Bahá*

287

When the ocean of My presence hath ebbed and the Book of My Revelation is ended, turn your faces toward Him Whom God hath purposed, Who hath branched from this Ancient Root.

—*Bahá'u'lláh*

288

He ['Abdu'l-Bahá] is, and should for all time be regarded, first and foremost, as the Center and Pivot of Bahá'u'lláh's peerless and all-enfolding Covenant, His most exalted handiwork, the stainless Mirror of His light, the perfect Exemplar of His teachings, the unerring Interpreter of His Word, the embodiment of every Bahá'í ideal. . . .

—*Shoghi Effendi*

289

The message of the holy, divine Manifestations is love; the phenomena of creation are based upon love; the radiance of the world is due to love; the well-being and happiness of the world depend upon it. Therefore, I admonish you that you must strive throughout the human world to diffuse the light of love. The people of this world are thinking of warfare; you must be peacemakers. The nations are self-centered; you must be thoughtful of others rather than yourselves. They are neglectful; you must be mindful. They are asleep; you should be awake and alert. May each one of you be as a shining star in the horizon of eternal glory. This is my wish for you and my highest hope.

—*'Abdu'l-Bahá*

290

Say: Rejoice not in the things ye possess; tonight they are yours, tomorrow others will possess them. Thus warneth you He Who is the All-Knowing, the All-Informed.

—*Bahá'u'lláh*

291

Happy the days that have been consecrated to the remembrance of God, and blessed the hours which have been spent in praise of Him Who is the All-Wise. By My life! Neither the pomp of the mighty, nor the wealth of the rich, nor even the ascendancy of the ungodly will endure. All will perish, at a word from Him. He, verily, is the All-Powerful, the All-Compelling, the Almighty. What advantage is there in the earthly things which men possess? That which shall profit them, they have utterly neglected. Erelong, they will awake from their slumber, and find themselves unable to obtain that which had escaped them in the days of their Lord, the Almighty, the All-Praised. Did they but know it, they would renounce their all, that their names may be mentioned before His throne.

—*Bahá'u'lláh*

292

Lament not in your hours of trial, neither rejoice therein; seek ye the Middle Way which is the remembrance of me in your afflictions and reflection over that which may befall you in future. Thus informeth you He Who is the Omniscient, He Who is aware.

—*Bahá'u'lláh*

293

We, verily, have made music as a ladder for your souls, a means whereby they may be lifted up unto the realm on high; make it not, therefore, as wings to self and passion.

—*Bahá'u'lláh*

294

O people of God! That which traineth the world is Justice, for it is upheld by two pillars, reward and punishment. These two pillars are the sources of life to the world.

—*Bahá'u'lláh*

295

Take ye counsel together in all matters, inasmuch as consultation is the lamp of guidance which leadeth the way, and is the bestower of understanding.

—*Bahá'u'lláh*

296

The shining spark of truth cometh forth only after the clash of differing opinions.

—*'Abdu'l-Bahá*

297

In this day, assemblies of consultation are of the greatest importance and a vital necessity. Obedience unto them is essential and obligatory. The members thereof must take counsel together in such wise that no occasion for ill-feeling or discord may arise.

—*'Abdu'l-Bahá*

298

Consultation must have for its object the investigation of truth. He who expresses an opinion should not voice it as correct and right but set it forth as a contribution to the consensus of opinion, for the light of reality becomes apparent when two opinions coincide. A spark is produced when flint and steel come together. Man should weigh his opinions with the utmost serenity, calmness and composure. Before expressing his own views he should carefully consider the views already advanced by others. If he finds that a previously expressed opinion is more true and worthy, he should accept it immediately and not willfully hold to an opinion of his own. By this excellent method he endeavors to arrive at unity and truth.

—*'Abdu'l-Bahá*

299

The prime requisites for them that take counsel together are purity of motive, radiance of spirit, detachment from all else save God, attraction to His Divine Fragrances, humility and lowliness amongst

His loved ones, patience and long-suffering in difficulties and servitude to His exalted Threshold.

—'Abdu'l-Bahá

300

True consultation is spiritual conference in the attitude and atmosphere of love. Members must love each other in the spirit of fellowship in order that good results may be forthcoming. Love and fellowship are the foundation.

—'Abdu'l-Bahá

301

It is seemly that the servant should, after each prayer, supplicate God to bestow mercy and forgiveness upon his parents. Thereupon God's call will be raised: "Thousand upon thousand of what thou hast asked for thy parents shall be thy recompense!" Blessed is he who remembereth his parents when communing with God.

—The Báb

302

O Son of Man!

Divest not thyself of My beauteous robe, and forfeit not thy portion from My wondrous fountain, lest thou shouldst thirst forevermore.

—Bahá'u'lláh

303

The spiritually learned are lamps of guidance among the nations, and stars of good fortune shining from the horizons of humankind. They are fountains of life for such as lie in the death of ignorance and unawareness, and clear springs of perfections for those who thirst and wander in the wasteland of their defects and errors. They are the dawning places of the emblems of Divine Unity and initiates in the mysteries of the glorious Qur'án. They are skilled physicians for the ailing body of the world, they are the sure antidote to the poison that has corrupted human society.

—*'Abdu'l-Bahá*

304

O Son of Being!
My love is My stronghold; he that entereth therein is safe and secure, and he that turneth away shall surely stray and perish.

—*Bahá'u'lláh*

305

Well is it with him who in every Dispensation recognizeth the Purpose of God for that Dispensation, and is not deprived therefrom by turning his gaze towards the things of the past.

—*The Báb*

306

God hath ordained that all the good things which lie in the treasury of His knowledge shall be attained through obedience unto Me, and every fire recorded in His Book, through disobedience unto Me.

—*The Báb*

307

With the utmost friendliness and in a spirit of perfect fellowship take ye counsel together, and dedicate the precious days of your lives to the betterment of the world and the promotion of the Cause of Him Who is the Ancient and Sovereign Lord of all.

—*Bahá'u'lláh*

308

Say: Follow, O people, what hath been prescribed unto you in Our Tablets, and walk not after the imaginations which the sowers of mischief have devised, they that commit wickedness. . . .

—*Bahá'u'lláh*

309

Say: O ye lovers of the One true God! Strive, that ye may truly recognize and know Him, and observe befittingly His precepts.

—*Bahá'u'lláh*

310

The time foreordained unto the peoples and kindreds of the earth is now come. The promises of God, as recorded in the holy Scriptures, have all been fulfilled. Out of Zion hath gone forth the Law of God, and Jerusalem, and the hills and the land thereof, are filled with the glory of His Revelation. Happy is the man that pondereth in his heart that which hath been revealed in the Books of God, the Help in Peril, the Self-Subsisting.

—*Bahá'u'lláh*

311

It behooveth the loved ones of the Lord to be the signs and tokens of His universal mercy and the embodiments of His own excelling grace. Like the sun, let them cast their rays upon garden and rubbish heap alike, and even as clouds in spring, let them shed down their rain upon flower and thorn. Let them seek but love and faithfulness, let them not follow the ways of unkindness, let their talk be confined to the secrets of friendship and of peace. Such are the attributes of the righteous, such is the distinguishing mark of those who serve His Threshold.

—*'Abdu'l-Bahá*

312

Verily I say, the tongue is for mentioning what is good, defile it not with unseemly talk. God hath forgiven what is past. Henceforward everyone should utter that which is meet and seemly, and should refrain from slander, abuse and whatever causeth sadness in men.

—*Bahá'u'lláh*

313

The Promised Day is come and the Lord of Hosts hath appeared. Rejoice ye with great joy by reason of this supreme felicity. Aid Him then through the power of wisdom and utterance. Thus biddeth you the One Who hath ever proclaimed, "Verily, no God is there but Me, the All-Knowing, the All-Wise."

—*Bahá'u'lláh*

314

He Whose advent hath been foretold in the heavenly Scriptures is come, could ye but understand it. The world's horizon is illumined by the splendors of this Most Great Revelation. Haste ye with radiant hearts and be not of them that are bereft of understanding. The appointed Hour hath struck and mankind is laid low. Unto this bear witness the honored servants of God.

—*Bahá'u'lláh*

315

Among the greatest of all services that can possibly be rendered by man to Almighty God is the education and training of children . . . so that these children, fostered by grace in the way of salvation, growing like pearls of divine bounty in the shell of education, will one day bejewel the crown of abiding glory.

It is, however, very difficult to undertake this service, even harder to succeed in it. I hope that thou wilt acquit thyself well in this most important of tasks, and successfully carry the day, and become an ensign of God's abounding grace; that these children, reared one and all in the holy Teachings, will develop natures like unto the sweet airs that blow across the gardens of the All-Glorious, and will waft their fragrance around the world.

—*'Abdu'l-Bahá*

316

Ye should consider the question of goodly character as of the first importance. It is incumbent upon every father and mother to counsel their children over a long period, and guide them unto those things which lead to everlasting honor.

—*'Abdu'l-Bahá*

317

Training in morals and good conduct is far more important than book learning. A child that is cleanly, agreeable, of good character, well-behaved—even though he be ignorant—is preferable to a child that is rude, unwashed, ill-natured, and yet becoming deeply versed in all the sciences and arts. The reason for this is that the child who conducts himself well, even though he be ignorant, is of benefit to others, while an ill-natured, ill-behaved child is corrupted and harmful to others, even though he be learned. If, however, the child be trained to be both learned and good, the result is light upon light.

—*'Abdu'l-Bahá*

318

It behooveth thee to sever thyself from all desires save thy Lord, the Supreme, expecting no help or aid from anyone in the universe, not even from thy father or children. Resign thyself to God! Content thyself with but little of this world's goods! Verily, economy is a great treasure.

—*'Abdu'l-Bahá*

319

It will not be possible in the future for men to amass great fortunes by the labors of others. The rich will willingly divide. They will come to this gradually, naturally, by their own volition. It will never be accomplished by war and bloodshed.

—*'Abdu'l-Bahá*

320

O Son of Being!
If poverty overtake thee, be not sad; for in time the Lord of wealth shall visit thee. Fear not abasement, for glory shall one day rest on thee.

—*Bahá'u'lláh*

321

Happiness consists of two kinds; physical and spiritual. The physical happiness is limited; its utmost duration is one day, one month, one year. It hath no result. Spiritual happiness is eternal and unfathomable. This kind of happiness appeareth in one's soul with the love of God and suffereth one to attain to the virtues and perfections of the world of humanity. Therefore, endeavor as much as thou art able in order to illumine the lamp of thy heart by the light of love.

—*'Abdu'l-Bahá*

322

O Son of Light!
Forget all save Me and commune with My spirit. This is of the essence of My command, therefore turn unto it.

—Bahá'u'lláh

323

Be generous in prosperity, and thankful in adversity. . . . Be a treasure to the poor, an admonisher to the rich, an answerer of the cry of the needy, a preserver of the sanctity of thy pledge.

—Bahá'u'lláh

324

All majesty and glory, O my God, and all dominion and light and grandeur and splendor be unto Thee. Thou bestowest sovereignty on whom Thou willest and dost withhold it from whom Thou desirest. No God is there by Thee, the All-Possessing, the Most Exalted. Thou art He Who createth from naught the universe and all that dwell therein. There is nothing worthy of Thee except Thyself, while all else but thee are as outcasts in Thy holy presence and are as nothing when compared to the glory of Thine Own Being.

— The Báb

325

Whatever hath befallen you, hath been for the sake of God. This is the truth, and in this there is no doubt. You should, therefore, leave all your affairs in His Hands, place your trust in Him, and rely upon Him. He will assuredly not forsake you. In this, likewise, there is no doubt.

—*Bahá'u'lláh*

326

God grant that the light of unity may envelope the whole earth, and that the seal, "the Kingdom is God's," may be stamped upon the brow of all its peoples.

—*Bahá'u'lláh*

327

True civilization will unfurl its banner in the midmost heart of the world whenever a certain number of its distinguished and high-minded sovereigns—the shining exemplars of devotion and determination—shall, for the good and happiness of all mankind, arise, with firm resolve and clear vision, to establish the Cause of Universal Peace.

—*'Abdu'l-Bahá*

328

O Son of Being!
Love Me, that I may love thee. If thou lovest Me not, My love can in no wise reach thee. Know this, O servant.

—Bahá'u'lláh

329

O rulers of the earth! Be reconciled among yourselves, that ye may need no more armaments save in a measure to safeguard your territories and dominions. Beware lest ye disregard the counsel of the All-Knowing, the Faithful.

Be united, O kings of the earth, for thereby will the tempest of discord be stilled amongst you, and your peoples find rest, if ye be of them that comprehend. Should anyone among you take up arms against another, rise ye all against him, for this is naught but manifest justice.

—Bahá'u'lláh

330

Today, this Servant has assuredly come to vivify the world and to bring into unity all who are on the face of the earth. That which God willeth shall come to pass and thou shalt see the earth even as the Abhá (Most Glorious) Paradise.

—Bahá'u'lláh

331

The world in the past has been ruled by force, and man has dominated over woman by reason of his more forceful and aggressive qualities both of body and mind. But the balance is already shifting; force is losing its dominance, and mental alertness, intuition, and the spiritual qualities of love and service, in which woman is strong, are gaining ascendancy.

—*'Abdu'l-Bahá*

332

Humanity is like a bird with its two wings—the one is male, the other female. Unless both wings are strong and impelled by some common force, the bird cannot fly heavenwards.

—*'Abdu'l-Bahá*

333

Women have equal rights with men upon earth; in religion and society they are a very important element. As long as women are prevented from attaining their highest possibilities, so long will men be unable to achieve the greatness which might be theirs.

—*'Abdu'l-Bahá*

334

Women must go on advancing; they must extend their knowledge of science, literature, history, for the perfection of humanity. Erelong they will receive their rights.

—'Abdu'l-Bahá

335

The days when idle worship was deemed sufficient are ended. The time is come when naught but the purest motive, supported by deeds of stainless purity, can ascend to the throne of the Most High and be acceptable unto Him.

— The Báb

336

Unto every father hath been enjoined the instruction of his son and daughter in the art of reading and writing and in all that hath been laid down in the Holy Tablet.

—Bahá'u'lláh

337

How vast the number of people who are well versed in every science, yet it is their adherence to the holy Word of God which will determine their faith, inasmuch as the fruit of every science is none other than the knowledge of divine precepts and submission unto His good-pleasure

— The Báb

338

O Son of Spirit!
I created thee rich, why dost thou bring thyself down to poverty? Noble I made thee, wherewith dost thou abase thyself? Out of the essence of knowledge I gave thee being, why seekest thou enlightenment from anyone beside Me? Out of the clay of love I molded thee, how dost thou busy thyself with another? Turn thy sight unto thyself, that thou mayest find Me standing within thee, mighty, powerful and self-subsisting.

—*Bahá'u'lláh*

339

The fundamentals of the whole economic condition are divine in nature and are associated with the world of the heart and spirit. . . .

Strive, therefore, to create love in the hearts in order that they may become glowing and radiant. . . . When the love of God is established, everything else will be realized. This is the true foundation of all economics.

—*'Abdu'l-Bahá*

340

The days of your life flee away as a breath of wind, and all your pomp and glory shall be folded up as were the pomp and glory of those gone before you.

—*Bahá'u'lláh*

341

O Son of Man!

Should prosperity befall thee, rejoice not, and should abasement come upon thee, grieve not, for both shall pass away and be no more.

—*Bahá'u'lláh*

342

The solution of economic questions will not be brought about by array of capital against labor, and labor against capital, in strife and conflict, but by the voluntary attitude of goodwill on both sides. Then a real and lasting justness of conditions will be secured. . . .

—*'Abdu'l-Bahá*

343

O Son of Man!

Bestow My wealth upon My poor, that in heaven thou mayest draw from stores of unfading splendor and treasures of imperishable glory. But by My life! To offer up thy soul is a more glorious thing couldst thou but see with Mine eye.

—*Bahá'u'lláh*

344

Today one of the chief causes of the differences in Europe is the diversity of languages. We say this man is a German, the other is an Italian, then we meet an Englishman and then again a Frenchman. Although they belong to the same race, yet language is the greatest barrier between them. Were a universal auxiliary language in operation they would all be considered as one.

—*'Abdu'l-Bahá*

345

The day is approaching when all the peoples of the world will have adopted one universal language and one common script. When this is achieved, to whatsoever city a man may journey, it shall be as if he were entering his own home.

—*Bahá'u'lláh*

346

In a time to come, morals will degenerate to an extreme degree. It is essential that children be reared in the Bahá'í way, that they may find happiness both in this world and the next. If not, they shall be beset by sorrows and troubles, for human happiness is founded upon spiritual behavior.

—*'Abdu'l-Bahá*

347

By Thy sovereignty, O Thou Who art glorified in the hearts of men! I have turned to Thee, forsaking mine own will and desire, that Thy holy will and pleasure may rule within me and direct me according to that which the pen of Thy eternal decree hath destined for me.

—*Bahá'u'lláh*

348

Gather the people around this Word that hath made the pebbles to cry out: "The Kingdom is God's, the Dawning-place of all signs!"

—*Bahá'u'lláh*

349

Know that nothing will benefit thee in this life save supplication and invocation unto God, service in His vineyard, and, with a heart full of love, be in constant servitude unto Him.

—*'Abdu'l-Bahá*

350

Waste not your time in idleness and sloth. Occupy yourselves with that which profiteth yourselves and others. Thus hath it been decreed in this Tablet from whose horizon the daystar of wisdom and utterance shineth resplendent.

The most despised of men in the sight of God are those who sit idly and beg. Hold ye fast unto the cord of material means, placing your whole trust in God, the Provider of all means.

—Bahá'u'lláh

351

It is enjoined upon every one of you to engage in some form of occupation, such as crafts, trades and the like. We have graciously exalted your engagement in such work to the rank of worship unto God, the True One. Ponder ye in your hearts the grace and the blessings of God and render thanks unto Him at eventide and at dawn.

—Bahá'u'lláh

352

Say: True liberty consisteth in man's submission unto My commandments, little as ye know it.

—Bahá'u'lláh

353

Knowledge is love. Study, listen to exhortations, think, try to understand the wisdom and greatness of God. The soil must be fertilized before the seed can be sown.

—'Abdu'l-Bahá

354

Do not despair! Work steadily. Sincerity and love will conquer hate. How many seemingly impossible events are coming to pass in these days! Set your faces steadily towards the Light of the World. Show love to all; "Love is the breath of the Holy Spirit in the heart of Man." Take courage! God never forsakes His children who strive and work and pray!

—*'Abdu'l-Bahá*

355

The source of all learning is the knowledge of God, exalted be His Glory, and this cannot be attained save through the knowledge of His Divine Manifestation.

—*Bahá'u'lláh*

356

In truth, knowledge is a veritable treasure for man, and a source of glory, of bounty, of joy, of exaltation, of cheer and gladness unto him.

—*Bahá'u'lláh*

357

In accordance with the divine teachings the acquisition of sciences and the perfection of arts are considered acts of worship. If a man engages with all his power in the acquisition of a science or in the perfection of an art, it is as if he has been worshipping God in churches and temples.

—*'Abdu'l-Bahá*

358

Men who suffer not, attain no perfection. The plant most pruned by the gardeners is that one which, when the summer comes, will have the most beautiful blossoms and the most abundant fruit.

—*'Abdu'l-Bahá*

359

The laborer cuts up the earth with his plough, and from that earth comes the rich and plentiful harvest. The more a man is chastened, the greater is the harvest of spiritual virtues shown forth by him. A soldier is no good General until he has been in the front of the fiercest battle and has received the deepest wounds.

—*'Abdu'l-Bahá*

360

O Son of Man!

Wert thou to speed through the immensity of space and traverse the expanse of heaven, yet thou wouldst find no rest save in submission to Our command and humbleness before Our Face.

—*Bahá'u'lláh*

361

Confession of sins and transgressions before human beings is not permissible, as it hath never been nor will ever be conducive to divine forgiveness. Moreover such confession before people results in one's humiliation and abasement, and God—exalted be His glory—wisheth not the humiliation of His servants.

—*Bahá'u'lláh*

362

O Son of Being!
Walk in My statutes for love of Me and deny thyself that which thou desirest if thou seekest My pleasure.

—*Bahá'u'lláh*

363

Humility exalteth man to the heaven of glory and power, whilst pride abaseth him to the depths of wretchedness and degradation.

—*Bahá'u'lláh*

364

According to the direct and sacred command of God we are forbidden to utter slander, are commanded to show forth peace and amity, are exhorted to rectitude of conduct, straightforwardness and harmony with all the kindreds and peoples of the world. We must obey and be the well-wishers of the governments of the land, regard disloyalty unto a just king as disloyalty to God Himself and wishing evil to the government a transgression of the Cause of God.

—*'Abdu'l-Bahá*

365

O Thou kind Lord! This gathering is turning to Thee. These hearts are radiant with Thy love. These minds and spirits are exhilarated by the message of Thy glad-tidings. O God! Let this American democracy become glorious in spiritual degrees even as it has aspired to material degrees, and render this just government victorious. Confirm this revered nation to upraise the standard of the oneness of humanity, to promulgate the Most Great Peace, to become thereby most glorious and praiseworthy among all the nations of the world. O God! This American nation is worthy of Thy favors and is deserving of Thy mercy. Make it precious and near to Thee through Thy bounty and bestowal.

—*'Abdu'l-Bahá*

366

Say: Think ye that your allegiance to His Cause can ever profit Him, or your repudiation of its truth cause Him any loss? No, by My Self, the All-Subduing, the Inaccessible, the Most High!

—*Bahá'u'lláh*

367

Rejoice, for the heavenly table is prepared for you.

Rejoice, for the angels of heaven are your assistants and helpers.

Rejoice, for the glance of the Blessed Beauty, Bahá'u'lláh, is directed upon you.

Rejoice, for Bahá'u'lláh is your Protector.

Rejoice, for the everlasting glory is destined for you.

Rejoice, for the eternal life is awaiting you.

—*'Abdu'l-Bahá*

368

Arise, in My Name, amongst My servants, and say: "O ye peoples of the earth! Turn yourselves towards Him Who hath turned towards you. He, verily, is the Face of God amongst you, and His Testimony and His Guide unto you. He hath come to you with signs which none can produce."

—*Bahá'u'lláh*

369

To read one verse, or even one word, in a spirit of joy and radiance, is preferable to the perusal of many Books.

—*Bahá'u'lláh*

370

Be in perfect unity. Never become angry with one another. . . . Love the creatures for the sake of God and not for themselves. You will never become angry or impatient if you love them for the sake of God.

—*'Abdu'l-Bahá*

371

All must be considered as submerged in the ocean of God's mercy. We must associate with all humanity in gentleness and kindliness. We must love all with love of the heart.

—*'Abdu'l-Bahá*

372

Beware lest ye harm any soul, or make any heart to sorrow; lest ye wound any man with your words, be he known to you or a stranger, be he friend or foe. Pray ye for all; ask ye that all be blessed, all be forgiven.

—*'Abdu'l-Bahá*

373

O beloved of the Lord! If any soul speak ill of an absent one, the only result will clearly be this: he will dampen the zeal of the friends and tend to make them indifferent. For backbiting is divisive, it is the leading cause among the friends of a disposition to withdraw. If any individual should speak ill of one who is absent, it is incumbent on his hearers, in a spiritual and friendly manner, to stop him, and say in effect: would this detraction serve any useful purpose?

—*'Abdu'l-Bahá*

374

We, verily, have decreed in Our Book a goodly and bountiful reward to whosoever will turn away from wickedness and lead a chaste and godly life.

—*Bahá'u'lláh*

375

We verily behold your actions. If We perceive from them the sweet smelling savor of purity and holiness, We will most certainly bless you.

—*Bahá'u'lláh*

376

All men have proceeded from God and unto Him shall all return. All shall appear before Him for judgment. He is the Lord of the Day of Resurrection, of Regeneration and of Reckoning, and His revealed Word is the Balance.

—*The Báb*

377

O Lord! Enable all the peoples of the earth to gain admittance into the Paradise of Thy Faith, so that no created being may remain beyond the bounds of Thy good-pleasure.

From time immemorial Thou has been potent to do what pleaseth Thee and transcendent above whatsoever Thou desirest.

—*The Báb*

378

Bahá'í marriage is the commitment of the two parties one to the other, and their mutual attachment of mind and heart. Each must, however, exercise the utmost care to become thoroughly acquainted with the character of the other, that the binding covenant between them may be a tie that will endure forever. Their purpose must be this: to become loving companions and comrades and at one with each other for time and eternity. . . .

The true marriage of Bahá'ís is this, that husband and wife should be united both physically and spiritually, that they may ever improve the spiritual life of each other, and may enjoy everlasting unity throughout all the worlds of God. This is Bahá'í marriage.

—*'Abdu'l-Bahá*

379

As for the question regarding marriage under the Law of God: first thou must choose one who is pleasing to thee, and then the matter is subject to the consent of father and mother. Before thou makest thy choice, they have no right to interfere.

—*'Abdu'l-Bahá*

380

And when He [God] desired to manifest grace and beneficence to men, and to set the world in order, He revealed observances and created laws; among them He established the law of marriage, made it as a fortress for well-being and salvation, and enjoined it upon us in that which was sent down out of the heaven of sanctity in His Most Holy Book.

—*Bahá'u'lláh*

381

Study the sciences, acquire more and more knowledge. Assuredly one may learn to the end of one's life! Use your knowledge always for the benefit of others; so may war cease on the face of this beautiful earth, and a glorious edifice of peace and concord be raised. Strive that your high ideals may be realized in the Kingdom of God on earth, as they will be in Heaven.

—*'Abdu'l-Bahá*

382

The tabernacle of unity hath been raised; regard ye not one another as strangers. Ye are the fruits of one tree, and the leaves of one branch.

—*Bahá'u'lláh*

383

Bahá'u'lláh has said, "If religion and faith are the causes of enmity and sedition, it is far better to be nonreligious, and the absence of religion would be preferable; for we desire religion to be the cause of amity and fellowship. If enmity and hatred exist, irreligion is preferable."

—*'Abdu'l-Bahá*

384

Economy is the foundation of human prosperity. The spendthrift is always in trouble. Prodigality on the part of any person is an unpardonable sin. We must never live on others like a parasitic plant. Every person must have a profession, whether it be literary or manual, and must live a clean, manly, honest life, an example of purity to be imitated by others. It is more kingly to be satisfied with a crust of stale bread than to enjoy a sumptuous dinner of many courses, the money for which comes out of the pockets of others. The mind of a contented person is always peaceful and his heart at rest.

—*'Abdu'l-Bahá*

385

Great is the blessedness awaiting the poor that endure patiently and conceal their sufferings. . . .

Please God, the poor may exert themselves and strive to earn the means of livelihood. This is a duty which, in this most great Revelation, hath been prescribed unto every one. . . .

—*Bahá'u'lláh*

386

The only real difference that exists between people is that they are at various stages of development. Some are imperfect—these must be brought to perfection. Some are asleep—they must be awakened; some are negligent—they must be roused; but one and all are the children of God. Love them all with your whole heart; no one is a stranger to the other, all are friends.

—*'Abdu'l-Bahá*

387

Fair speech and truthfulness, by reason of their lofty rank and position, are regarded as a sun shining above the horizon of knowledge.

—*Bahá'u'lláh*

388

Praise be unto Thee, O our God, that Thou hast sent down unto us that which draweth us nigh unto Thee, and supplieth us with every good thing sent down by Thee in Thy Books and Thy Scriptures. Protect us, we beseech Thee, O my Lord, from the hosts of idle fancies and vain imaginations. Thou, in truth, art the Mighty, the All-Knowing.

—*Bahá'u'lláh*

389

The peoples of the world are fast asleep. Were they to wake from their slumber, they would hasten with eagerness unto God, the All-Knowing, the All-Wise.

—*Bahá'u'lláh*

390

Charity is pleasing and praiseworthy in the sight of God and is regarded as a prince among goodly deeds. Consider ye and call to mind that which the All-Merciful hath revealed in the Qur'án: "They prefer them before themselves, though poverty be their own lot. And with such as are preserved from their own covetousness shall it be well." Viewed in this light, the blessed utterance above is, in truth, the day-star of utterances. Blessed is he who preferreth his brother before himself. Verily, such a man is reckoned, by virtue of the Will of God, the All-Knowing, the All-Wise, with the people of Bahá who dwell in the Crimson Ark.

—Bahá'u'lláh

391

Vie ye with each other in the service of God and of His Cause. This is indeed what profiteth you in this world, and in that which is to come.

—Bahá'u'lláh

392

Happy the soul that shall forget his own good, and like the chosen ones of God, vie with his fellows in service to the good of all.

—'Abdu'l-Bahá

393

By God, the True One, verily, the gifts of God are in such profusion as to rush like a torrent, overflow as a sea, and shower as rain. Gird up thy loins, strengthen thy back, make firm thy feet, and exert thyself in quickening souls, dilating breasts, illumining insights, giving hearing to ears, and attracting hearts. Unseal the jars of the choice wine of the love of God, and give the craving ones to drink from this cup which is overflowing with the knowledge of God.

—'Abdu'l-Bahá

394

Know ye that the poor are the trust of God in your midst. Watch that ye betray not His trust, that ye deal not unjustly with them and that ye walk not in the ways of the treacherous.

—*Bahá'u'lláh*

395

O thou spiritual friend! . . . Know thou that prayer is indispensable and obligatory, and man under no pretext whatsoever is excused from performing the prayer unless he be mentally unsound, or an insurmountable obstacle prevent him.

—*'Abdu'l-Bahá*

396

I bear witness, O my God, that Thou hast created me to know Thee and to worship Thee. I testify, at this moment, to my powerlessness and to Thy might, to my poverty and to Thy wealth.

There is none other God but Thee, the Help in Peril, the Self-Subsisting.

—*Bahá'u'lláh*

397

If it be Thy pleasure, make me to grow as a tender herb in the meadows of Thy grace, that the gentle winds of Thy will may stir me up and bend me into conformity with Thy pleasure, in such wise that my movement and my stillness may be wholly directed by Thee.

—Bahá'u'lláh

398

The source of all good is trust in God, submission unto His command, and contentment with His holy will and pleasure. . . .

The source of all glory is acceptance of whatsoever the Lord hath bestowed, and contentment with that which God hath ordained.

—Bahá'u'lláh

399

O Son of Man!
Upon the tree of effulgent glory I have hung for thee the choicest fruits, wherefore hast thou turned away and contented thyself with that which is less good? Return then unto that which is better for thee in the realm on high.

—Bahá'u'lláh

400

God hath prescribed unto every one the duty of teaching His Cause. Whoever ariseth to discharge this duty, must needs, ere he proclaimeth His Message, adorn himself with the ornament of an upright and praiseworthy character, so that his words may attract the hearts of such as are receptive to his call. Without it, he can never hope to influence his hearers.

—*Bahá'u'lláh*

401

Whoso openeth his lips in this Day and maketh mention of the name of his Lord, the hosts of Divine inspiration shall descend upon him from the heaven of My name, the All-Knowing, the All-Wise.

—*Bahá'u'lláh*

402

Know thou the value of these days; let not this chance escape thee. Beg thou God to make thee a lighted candle, so that thou mayest guide a great multitude through this darksome world.

—'Abdu'l-Bahá

403

O Son of Being!
Make mention of Me on My earth, that in My heaven I may remember thee, thus shall Mine eyes and thine be solaced.

—*Bahá'u'lláh*

404

Verily the most necessary thing is contentment under all circumstances; by this one is preserved from morbid conditions and from lassitude. Yield not to grief and sorrow: they cause the greatest misery. Jealousy consumeth the body and anger doth burn the liver: avoid these two as you would a lion.

—*'Abdu'l-Bahá*

405

O Friends!
Verily I say, whatsoever ye have concealed within your hearts is to Us open and manifest as the day; but that it is hidden is of Our grace and favor, and not of your deserving.

—*Bahá'u'lláh*

406

O God, my God! Thou art my Hope and my Beloved, my highest Aim and Desire! With great humbleness and entire devotion I pray to Thee to make me a minaret of Thy love in Thy land, a lamp of Thy knowledge among Thy creatures, and a banner of divine bounty in Thy dominion.

Number me with such of Thy servants as have detached themselves from everything but Thee, have sanctified themselves from the transitory things of this world, and have freed themselves from the promptings of the voicers of idle fancies.

Let my heart be dilated with joy through the spirit of confirmation from Thy Kingdom, and brighten my eyes by beholding the hosts of divine assistance descending successively upon me from the kingdom of Thine omnipotent glory.

Thou art, in truth, the Almighty, the All-Glorious, the All-Powerful.

—*Bahá'u'lláh*

407

O my God! O my God! Thou seest me in my lowliness and weakness, occupied with the greatest undertaking, determined to raise Thy word among the masses and to spread Thy teachings among Thy peoples. How can I succeed unless Thou assist me with the breath of the Holy Spirit, help me to triumph by the hosts of Thy glorious kingdom, and shower upon me Thy confirmations, which alone can change a gnat into an eagle, a drop of water into rivers and seas, and an atom into lights and suns?

—*'Abdu'l-Bahá*

408

The Divine Springtime is come, O Most Exalted Pen, for the Festival of the All-Merciful is fast approaching. Bestir thyself, and magnify, before the entire creation, the name of God, and celebrate His praise, in such wise that all created things may be regenerated and made new.

—*Bahá'u'lláh*

409

The winds of the true springtide are passing over you; adorn yourselves with blossoms like trees in the scented garden. Spring clouds are streaming; then turn you fresh and verdant like the sweet eternal fields. The dawn star is shining, set your feet on the true path. The sea of might is swelling, hasten to the shores of high resolve and fortune. The pure water of life is welling up, why wear away your days in a desert of thirst? Aim high, choose noble ends.

—*'Abdu'l-Bahá*

List of Abbreviations

Passages from the Bahá'í writings found in this compilation come from many sources. A list of abbreviations follows.

ABL	'Abdu'l-Bahá in London
ADJ	The Advent of Divine Justice
BE	Bahá'í Education
BM	Bahá'í Meetings and the Nineteen Day Feast
BNE	Bahá'u'lláh and the New Era
BP	Bahá'í Prayers
CC 1	The Compilation of Compilations, vol. 1.
CC 2	The Compilation of Compilations, vol. 2.
CL	Century of Light
DB	The Dawn-Breakers
ESW	Epistle to the Son of the Wolf
GDM	Gems of Divine Mysteries
GL	Gleanings from the Writings of Bahá'u'lláh
HWA	The Hidden Words, Arabic
HWP	The Hidden Words, Persian
KA	The Kitáb-i-Aqdas: The Most Holy Book
KI	The Kitáb-i-Íqán: The Book of Certitude
PM	Prayers and Meditations

PT	Paris Talks
PUP	The Promulgation of Universal Peace
SAB	Selections from the Writings of 'Abdu'l-Bahá
SAQ	Some Answered Questions.
SDC	The Secret of Divine Civilization
SLH	The Summons of the Lord of Hosts: Tab lets of Bahá'u'lláh
SWB	Selections from the Writings of the Báb (2006)
TAB	Tablets of Abdul-Baha Abbas
TB	Tablets of Bahá'u'lláh revealed after the Kitáb-i-Aqdas
TU	The Tabernacle of Unity
WOB	The World Order of Bahá'u'lláh: Selected Letters
WT	Will and Testament of 'Abdu'l-Bahá

References

Each reference has three parts: 1) the extract number, 2) an abbreviation for the work the passage comes from, and 3) a page number, passage number, or paragraph number.

1. PUP 13
2. PUP 52
3. GL 43.5
4. KI ¶118–19
5. TB 35–36
6. GL 111.1
7. PT 1.9
8. PT 1.7
9. PT 1.10
10. TB 138
11. KA Q&A 106
12. TU 1.9
13. PUP 639
14. TAB 277
15. GL 136.6
16. KA ¶58
17. ESW 14
18. GL 4.1–2
19. GL 146.1
20. SAB 7.2
21. ESW 29
22. GL 43.4
23. PT 49.10–11
24. SAB 100.2
25. GL 110.1
26. PUP 86
27. HWA no. 31
28. BP 185
29. HWA no. 8
30. SAB 178.1
31. PT 14.7
32. PUP 346
33. GL 27.2
34. ESW 30

35. HWP no. 64
36. GL 66.6
37. GL 14.16
38. GL 128.9
39. SAQ 163
40. TB 12–13
41. PM 4
42. GL 132.5
43. SWB 2.24.2
44. PT 41.7
45. PT 18.6
46. BP 175–76
47. GL 5.1
48. GL 7.1
49. BP 19–20
50. GL 14.16
51. SLH 1.192
52. TU 1.2
53. HWA no. 44
54. TB 156
55. GPB 220
56. GPB 220
57. KI ¶177
58. ESW 21
59. HWP no. 5
56. PT 26.9
61. KI ¶1
62. KI ¶2
63. KA ¶78
64. SLH 1.102
65. SLH 1.136
66. HWA no. 3
67. GL 100.4
68. TB 71
69. GL 96.3
70. TB 156
71. TAB 546
72. GL 43.3
73. GL 23.1
74. HWA no. 64
75. TB 155
76. GPB 21
77. KA ¶3
78. KA ¶1
79. HWA no. 66
80. HWP no. 15
81. PUP 458
82. KA ¶53
83. GL 45.1
84. PM 95
85. PT 25.18–19
86. HWA no. 50
87. HWA no. 55
88. TU 2.35

89. BM 3
90. GL 43.8
91. GL 70.2
92. TB 173
93. PUP 638–39
94. BP 113
95. TU 1.1
96. TB 188
97. SAB 172.1
98. CC 2:232
99. PT 54.8
100. PT 54.9–12
101. GL 5.6
102. GL 5.5
103. SAB 71.1
104. PT 5.24–25
105. TU 5.7
106. GL 83.1
107. GDM 46
108. PUP 304
109. BP 87
110. PUP 301
111. HWP no. 80
112. SLH 5:44
113. ESW 26
114. PT 51.11
115. ABL 79
116. TAB 62
117. BE 8
118. TAB 579
119. TAB 87
120. TAB 580
121. SAB 227.18
122. PT 50.11
123. GL 66.6
124. TB 86
125. TB 36
126. PUP 304
127. TAB 136
128. TAB 45
129. HWP no. 25
130. ESW 30
131. DB 140–41
132. KI ¶128
133. GL 125.2
134. HWA no. 30
135. BP 138
136. GL 29.1
137. HWA no. 4
138. TB 101
139. KI ¶100
140. PUP 231
141. HWP no. 26
142. HWA no. 39

143. PUP 126
144. TB 129
145. DB 92
146. TB 156
147. TB 155
148. GL 34.6
149. HWA no. 52
150. SAQ 242–43
151. SLH 1.44
152. GL 22.8
153. ADJ ¶40
154. ESW 50
155. HWA no. 2
156. PUP 85
157. PUP 409
158. TB 26
159. HWP no. 53
160. PT 55.1
161. GL 117.1
162. HWP no. 51
163. PT 14.7–8
164. HWP no. 9
165. GL 82.1
166. HWA no. 8
167. SAQ 242
168. HWA no. 16
169. TAB 683
170. PUP 358–59
171. TAB 594
172. PT 57.3
173. HWA no. 25
174. HWP no. 55
175. HWA no. 67
176. KA ¶149
177. BP 114
178. DB 94
179. PT 21.6
180. HWA no. 45
181. SWB 6.11.3
182. HWA no. 46
183. BP 167
184. PM 108
185. TB 221–22.
186. PUP 128
187. PT 19.5
188. PT 18.3
189. SAQ 222
190. PT 15.7
191. PT 15.8–10
192. PT 58.1–3
193. KA ¶181
194. BP 98
195. ESW 56
196. WOB 104

197. GL 10.1
198. GL 103.3
199. PUP 26
200. PUP 170
201. PUP 299–300
202. PUP 237
203. PT 6.7
204. TU 5.5
205. TU 4.4
206. TU 4.6
207. TU 4.9
208. SAB 191.1
209. TU 4.8
210. SAB 194.2
211. SAB 31.15
212. PUP 215
213. SAB 29.4
214. WOB 203
215. WOB 203
216. WOB 204–5
217. ESW 27
218. GL 34.5
219. PT 7.7
220. PT 18.6
221. PT 9.1
222. TB 156
223. KI ¶213
224. GL 34.6
225. HWA no. 56
226. TB 68
227. HWA no. 27
228. GL 132.5
229. HWA no. 5
230. BP 213
231. PT 17.7
232. PUP 226–27
233. SAB 181.2
234. TB 156
235. SWB 1.5.9
236. BP 174–75
237. HWA no. 17
238. CC 1:202
239. TB 52
240. PUP 510
241. GL 120.3
242. PT 45.11
243. BP 226
244. PUP 276
245. GL 28.2
246. SLH 1:112
247. GL 111.1
248. SAB 35.8
249. GL 34.3
250. PUP 276

251. SAB 38.3
252. PUP 106
253. CC 2:232
254. SDC ¶194
255. GL 129.3
256. GL 155.2
257. SDC ¶130
258. GL 110.1
259. TB 48
260. PUP 328–29
261. HWA 68
262. PUP 267
263. PUP 638
264. BP 238
265. GL 117.1
266. PT 40.21
267. ABL 91
268. PM 87
269. GL 156.1
270. TAB 69
271. PUP 200
272. PUP 232–33
273. PT 45.11
274. ADJ ¶56
275. PUP 60–61
276. ESW 26
277. SAQ 130
278. PT 44.26
279. PUP 244
280. PUP 641
281. PM 272
282. CL 19
283. PUP 342
284. PUP 345–46
285. PT 34.8
286. PUP 544
287. KA ¶121
288. WOB 134
289. PUP 477
290. KA ¶40
291. KA ¶40
292. KA ¶43
293. KA ¶51
294. TB 27
295. TB 168
296. SAB 44.1
297. BA 21
298. PUP 99–100
299. BA 21
300. PUP 100
301. SWB 3.22.1
302. HWA no. 37
303. SDC ¶59
304. HWA no. 9

305. SWB 3.34.2
306. SWB 1.4.2
307. GL 92.3
308. GL 141.2
309. GL 3.2
310. GL 10.1
311. SAB 206.11
312. TB 219–20
313. TB 239–40
314. TB 244
315. SAB 106.1–2
316. SAB 108.1
317. SAB 110.2
318. TAB 97–98
319. BNE 145
320. HWA no. 53
321. TAB 673–74
322. HWA no. 16
323. ESW 93
324. BP 141–42
325. CC 1:171
326. GL 7.3
327. SDC ¶120
328. HWA no. 5
329. GL 119.4–5
330. BNE 156
331. BNE 149
332. BNE 147
333. PT 40.33
334. BNE 148–49
335. DB 93
336. TB 128
337. SWB 3.14.1
338. HWA no. 13
339. PUP 334–35
340. GL 71.3
341. HWA no. 52
342. BNE 144–45
343. HWA no. 57
344. BNE 164
345. GL 117.1
346. SAB 100.2
347. BP 171
348. KA ¶169
349. TAB 98
350. TB 26
351. TB 26
352. GL 159.4
353. CC 1:204
354. PT 6.12
355. TB 156
356. ESW 27
357. SAB 126.1
358. PT 14.9

359. PT 14.10
360. HWA no. 40
361. TB 24
362. HWA no. 38
363. ESW 30
364. WT 8
365. BP 26
366. GL 121.7
367. PUP 299
368. SLH 1.134
369. KA Q&A 68
370. PUP 128
371. PUP 86–87
372. SAB 35.11
373. SAB 193.8
374. GL 59.5
375. GL 141.4
376. SWB 6.8.1
377. SWB 7.21.1–2
378. SAB 86.1–2
379. SAB 85.1
380. BP 118
381. PT 11.13
382. GL 112.1
383. PUP 324
384. BNE 102
385. GL 100.4–5
386. PT 53.13
387. TB 40
388. BP 15
389. GL 71.2
390. TB 71
391. ADJ 126
392. SDC ¶208
393. TAB 163
394. SLH 5.11
395. TAB 683
396. BP 4
397. PM 240
398.TB 155
399. HWA no. 21
400. GL 158.1
401. GL 129.3
402. SAB 64.3
403. HWA no. 43
404. BNE 108
405. HWP no. 60
406. BP 56–57
407. BP 214
408. GL 14.1
409. SDC ¶186

Bibliography

Works of Bahá'u'lláh

Epistle to the Son of the Wolf. Translated by Shoghi Effendi. 1st pocket-size ed. Wilmette, IL: Bahá'í Publishing Trust, 1988.

Gems of Divine Mysteries: Javáhiru'l-Asrár. N.p.: Bahá'í Publications Australia, 2002.

Gleanings from the Writings of Bahá'u'lláh. New ed. Translated by Shoghi Effendi. Wilmette, IL: Bahá'í Publishing, 2005.

The Hidden Words. Translated by Shoghi Effendi. Wilmette, IL: Bahá'í Publishing, 2002.

The Kitáb-i-Aqdas: The Most Holy Book. 1st pocket-size ed. Wilmette, IL: Bahá'í Publishing Trust, 1993.

The Kitáb-i-Íqán: The Book of Certitude. Translated by Shoghi Effendi. Wilmette, IL: Bahá'í Publishing, 2003.

Prayers and Meditations. Translated from the original Persian and Arabic by Shoghi Effendi. First pocket-size ed. Wilmette, IL: Bahá'í Publishing Trust, 1987.

The Summons of the Lord of Hosts: Tablets of Bahá'u'lláh. Wilmette, IL: Bahá'í Publishing, 2006.

The Tabernacle of Unity: Bahá'u'lláh's Responses to Mánikchí Ṣáḥib and Other Writings. N.p.: Bahá'í World Centre, 2006.

Tablets of Bahá'u'lláh revealed after the Kitáb-i-Aqdas. Compiled by the Research Department of the Universal House of Justice. Translated by Habib Taherzadeh et al. Wilmette, IL: Bahá'í Publishing Trust, 1988.

Works of the Báb

Selections from the Writings of the Báb. Compiled by the Research Department of the Universal House of Justice. Translated by Habib Taherzadeh with the assistance of a committee at the Bahá'í World Center. Wilmette, IL: Bahá'í Publishing Trust, 2006.

Works of 'Abdu'l-Bahá

'Abdu'l-Bahá in London: Addresses and Notes of Conversations. [Compiled by Eric Hammond.] London: Longmans Green, 1912; reprinted Bahá'í Publishing Trust, 1982.

Paris Talks: Addresses Given by 'Abdu'l-Bahá in 1911. Wilmette, IL: Bahá'í Publishing, 2006.

The Promulgation of Universal Peace: Talks Delivered by 'Abdu'l-Bahá during His Visit to the United States and Canada in 1912. Compiled by Howard MacNutt. New ed. Wilmette, IL: Bahá'í Publishing Trust, 2007.

The Secret of Divine Civilization. 1st pocket-size ed. Translated by Marzieh Gail and Ali-Kuli Khan. Wilmette, IL: Bahá'í Publishing, 2007.

Selections from the Writings of 'Abdu'l-Bahá. Compiled by the Research Department of the Universal House of Justice. Translated by a Committee at the Bahá'í World Center and Marzieh Gail. Wilmette, IL: Bahá'í Publishing Trust, 1997.

Some Answered Questions. Compiled and translated by Laura Clifford Barney. 1st pocket-size ed. Wilmette, IL: Bahá'í Publishing Trust, 1984.

Tablets of Abdul-Baha Abbas. 3 vols. New York: Bahai Publishing Society, 1909–16.

Will and Testament of 'Abdu'l-Bahá. Wilmette, IL: Bahá'í Publishing Trust, 1944.

Works of Shoghi Effendi

The Advent of Divine Justice. New pocket-size ed. Wilmette, IL: Bahá'í Publishing Trust, 2006.

The World Order of Bahá'u'lláh: Selected Letters. 1st pocket-size ed. Wilmette, IL.: Bahá'í Publishing Trust, 1991.

Works of the Universal House of Justice

Century of Light. Wilmette, IL: Bahá'í Publishing Trust, 2001.

Compilations of Bahá'í Writings

Bahá'í Education: Extracts from the Writings of Bahá'u'lláh, 'Abdu'l-Bahá, and Shoghi Effendi. Compiled by the Research Department of the Universal House of Justice. Wilmette, IL: Bahá'í Publishing Trust, 1977.

Bahá'í Meetings and the Nineteen Day Feast: Extracts from the Writings of Bahá'u'lláh, 'Abdu'l-Bahá, and Shoghi Effendi. Compiled by the Universal House of Justice. Wilmette, IL: Bahá'í Publishing Trust, 1976.

Bahá'í Prayers: A Selection of Prayers Revealed by Bahá'u'lláh, the Báb, and 'Abdu'l-Bahá. Wilmette, IL: Bahá'í Publishing Trust, 2002.

The Compilation of Compilations: Prepared by the Universal House of Justice 1963–1990. 2 Vols. Australia: Bahá'í Publications Australia, 1991.

Other Works

Esslemont, J. E. *Bahá'u'lláh and the New Era: An Introduction to the Bahá'í Faith*. Wilmette, IL: Bahá'í Publishing, 2006.

Nabíl-i-A'ẓam [Muḥammad-i-Zarandí]. *The Dawn-Breakers: Nabíl's Narrative of the Early Days of the Bahá'í Revelation*. Translated and edited by Shoghi Effendi. Wilmette, IL: Bahá'í Publishing Trust, 1932.

Bahá'í PUBLISHING AND THE BAHÁ'Í FAITH

Bahá'í Publishing produces books based on the teachings of the Bahá'í Faith. Founded over 160 years ago, the Bahá'í Faith has spread to some 235 nations and territories and is now accepted by more than five million people. The word "Bahá'í" means "follower of Bahá'u'lláh." Bahá'u'lláh, the founder of the Bahá'í Faith, asserted that he is the Messenger of God for all of humanity in this day. The cornerstone of his teachings is the establishment of the spiritual unity of humankind, which will be achieved by personal transformation and the application of clearly identified spiritual principles. Bahá'ís also believe that there is but one religion and that all the Messengers of God—among them Abraham, Zoroaster, Moses, Krishna, Buddha, Jesus, and Muḥammad—have progressively revealed its nature. Together, the world's great religions are expressions of a single, unfolding divine plan. Human beings, not God's Messengers, are the source of religious divisions, prejudices, and hatreds.

The Bahá'í Faith is not a sect or denomination of another religion, nor is it a cult or a social movement. Rather, it is a globally recognized independent world religion founded on new books of scripture revealed by Bahá'u'lláh.

Bahá'í Publishing is an imprint of the National Spiritual Assembly of the Bahá'ís of the United States.

For more information about the Bahá'í Faith,
or to contact Bahá'ís near you, visit
http://www.bahai.us/
or call
1-800-22-UNITE

Other Books Available from Bahá'í Publishing

From a Gnat to an Eagle
The Story of Nathan Rutstein
by Nathan Rutstein
$18.00 U.S. / $20.00 CAN
Trade paper
ISBN-10: 1-931847-46-0
ISBN-13: 978-1-931847-46-9

From a Gnat to an Eagle is the story of Nathan Rutstein's life in his own humble words, a story of spiritual transformation and personal triumph.

The child of Jewish immigrants in the Bronx, Nathan Rutstein was raised in a home devoid of books and ran the streets with gangs as a youth. When he was admitted to college on a sports scholarship, he seemed headed for a career in baseball, but the pursuit of justice—particularly racial equality—motivated him to apply himself to his studies and aim for something nobler.

Unaware at first of his own spiritual nature, Nathan emerged from his youth with a deep thirst for personal spiritual growth rooted in the teachings of the Bahá'í Faith. Though nothing in his upbringing encouraged him to pursue the life of the mind, eventually he became an author, a teacher, and a tireless advocate for racial equality, which became the dominating passion of his life. The book is a compelling account of a remarkable man and an illuminating portrait of how a person can be transformed through the power of love, dedication, and perseverance in the path of personal spiritual development.

Illumine My Heart

Bahá'í Prayers for Every Occasion

by Bahá'u'lláh, the Báb, and 'Abdu'l-Bahá

$12.00 U.S. / $13.50 CAN

Trade paper

ISBN-10: 1-931847-53-3
ISBN-13: 978-1-931847-53-7

Illumine My Heart is a collection of prayers from the sacred writings of the Bahá'í Faith. The prayers included here will assist spiritual seekers to walk a spiritual path with practical feet, and to navigate the ups and downs of life with comfort and assurance. There are prayers that deal with the tests and difficulties we face in everyday life, prayers for healing and bereavement, prayers we can say for loved ones that have passed away, prayers for families and marriage, for young children, and for peace and unity. In *Illumine My Heart,* readers will find a wellspring of soul-stirring and uplifting words to accompany them on every stage of life's journey.

Remembering 1969

Searching for the Eternal in Changing Times

by Robert Atkinson

$19.00 U.S. / $21.00 CAN

Hardcover

ISBN-10: 1-931847-54-1
ISBN-13: 978-1-931847-54-4

Remembering 1969 is the story of one man's search for personal spiritual growth during the transitional times of the 1960s. Robert Atkinson offers a beautifully written portrait of a defining, transformative year in his young adult life and, in the process, tells the story of a generation in transition. Beginning on July 20, 1969, with Neil Armstrong's walk on the moon, Atkinson's journey merges with important events of the time, including Woodstock and the maiden voyage of the Hudson River sloop *Clearwater*. Atkinson works with Pete Seeger on the *Clearwater*, visits Arlo Guthrie at his home in the Berkshires, and serendipitously meets Joseph Campbell, who becomes an important mentor.

His memoir follows the cycle of the seasons, starting with summer and sailing on the sloop. Fall finds Atkinson in the woods on a solitary retreat, where he learns important lessons from being alone in nature. Winter carries him to a retreat at a Franciscan monastery to explore the mysteries of a sacred tradition. A fateful meeting with Joseph Campbell helps to put the entire journey into perspective. Spring brings a return to Atkinson's alma mater college to teach a course and share with students the timeless lessons he has learned, awakening in them their own spiritual unfolding.

WAITING FOR THE SUNRISE
ONE FAMILY'S STRUGGLE AGAINST GENOCIDE AND RACISM
by Elizabeth Gatorano
$19.00 U.S. / $21.00 CAN
Trade paper
ISBN-10: 1-931847-45-2
ISBN-13: 978-1-931847-45-2

Waiting for the Sunrise is the personal account of an interracial family's struggle against pervasive racism in the

U.S. and the horrors of the civil war that plagued Rwanda in 1994. Raised in the American Midwest, author Elizabeth Gatorano, who is White, had no idea of the trials she would face after marrying Phanuel, who is Black and an immigrant to the U.S. from Rwanda. Prejudice against their marriage and their family followed them and their children wherever they went, often making them the focus of racist discrimination and threats of violence at home and at work.

In 1994, when fighting broke out in Rwanda, both Liz and Phanuel worked diligently to bring as many members of his family to safety as they could. Yet the harrowing rescue of his family from Rwanda was only the beginning of the difficult journey that lay ahead. Faced with the challenge of adapting to a new culture in a foreign country, Phanuel's family struggled to adjust to life in the U.S. The relatives' gratitude gradually gave way to the fears and prejudices they brought with them from Rwanda, and Liz and Phanuel eventually found themselves the targets of suspicion and hate from the very people they had helped to save.

Throughout these ordeals, Liz and Phanuel responded to hostility with love and patience, their faith in each other and in God remaining unshakable, even in the darkest hours. After accepting the Bahá'í Faith, they became even more committed to helping the less fortunate and personifying the virtues of love and unity found in the writings of Bahá'u'lláh. Together, they overcame all obstacles in their path, and they continue to help those in need today.